Copper Harbor overlooks Lake Superior from Michigan's Keweenaw Peninsula.

THE GREAT LAKES

North America's Inland Sea

D1543194

Ken Dequaine

D M Kidd
6/15/75

THE
GREAT LAKES
North America's Inland Sea

BY THE EDITORS OF OUTDOOR WORLD

Publisher and Editorial Director: Michael P. Dineen
Executive Editor: Robert L. Polley
Managing Editor: John M. Nuhn
Text by Linda B. Myers

OUTDOOR WORLD
Waukesha, Wisconsin

October trees brighten the sandstone
formations of Devils Island in Lake Superior, part
of Apostle Islands National Lakeshore.

COUNTRY BEAUTIFUL: *Publisher and Editorial Director:* Michael P. Dineen; *Executive Editor:* Robert L. Polley; *Assistant Publisher:* John Huenink; *Executive Director:* Tom Patty; *Senior Editors:* Kenneth L. Schmitz, James H. Robb, Stewart L. Udall; *Art Director:* Buford Nixon; *Managing Editor:* John M. Nuhn: *Associate Editors:* D'Arlyn Marks, Kay Kundinger; *Contributing Editor:* Linda B. Myers; *Editorial Assistant:* Diana Durham; *Production Manager:* Donna Griesemer; *Administration:* Bruce L. Schneider.

Country Beautiful Corporation is a wholly owned subsidiary of Flick-Reedy Corporation: President: Frank Flick; Vice President and General Manager: Michael P. Dineen; Treasurer and Secretary: August Caamano.

ACKNOWLEDGEMENTS

The editors wish to express their gratitude to Mrs. William Whichello, Joe Kirkish, the Michigan Tourist Council, the Michigan Department of Natural Resources, the Wisconsin Department of Natural Resources and the U. S. Department of the Interior for their valuable assistance in the preparation of this book.

Pages 2-3: October colors decorate Devils Island, the northernmost part of Apostle Islands National Lakeshore in Wisconsin.

Michigan Tourist Council

CONTENTS

*The marina at Mackinac Island lures
yachts and sailboats from all over the Great
Lakes. On the rise above the docks, old
Fort Mackinac guards the island.*

AN AWAKENING

Hundreds of millions of years ago, boiling lava flows criss-crossed and hardened into the Minnesota north shore. Orange lichens and harebells cling to the ancient, weather-beaten boulders.

Ken Dequaine

A Gift of
the Glaciers

If you could condense all time into an hour, the Great Lakes would have been born in the last few seconds. As we know them today, the lakes are geological youngsters. But their story begins hundreds of millions of years ago. Then the land was drenched in molten lava, boiling up from the earth's core. This was the Pre-Cambrian Era which imprisoned the earth from the very beginning of its history (possibly 4.5 to 5 billion years ago) until approximately five hundred million years ago. When this volcanic age finally relinquished its hold, it left behind the foundation of the Great Lakes.

An ever-present reminder of Pre-Cambrian days are the tortured and broken rocks of the Canadian Shield. Left relatively visible through the sediments of subsequent geological eras, this massive formation, covering 2.8 million square miles from the Northwest Territories of Canada to the lands around Lake Superior, is among the oldest rock on earth. Most of the rich mineral deposits found in the Great Lakes region, including Minnesota iron and Michigan copper, are products of the Canadian Shield. So, too, is the rugged terrain that gives Lake Superior its stunning scenery.

The Paleozoic Era followed the Pre-Cambrian from 500 to 185 million years ago. Shallow seas oozed into the lake region, forming a checkerboard of land and swamps. An abundance of fossils indicates that life forms began to develop. Various periods of the Paleozoic identify the seas according to their extent and fossil varieties; during the earliest period, the Cambrian, marine waters spread invertebrate life forms across the interior of the United States and southern Ontario in the Great Lakes region. The next period, the Ordovician, added the first vertebrates and extended the warm seas over part of the Canadian Shield.

The Silurian Period, subsequent to the Ordovician, is responsible for one of the Great Lakes' most prominent geological formations. The Silurian waters deposited dolomite, a tough limestone, in a continuous layer which runs from New York State across Ontario into Michigan's Upper Peninsula (it forms the islands that hopscotch across Lake Huron, separating it from Georgian Bay) and then curves south along Lake Michigan through Wisconsin where it forms the Door Peninsula. This limestone layer is called the Niagara Escarpment because its tough back supports the magnificent falls that tumble toward Lake Ontario.

Glacial ice sheets paid their first call to Great Lakes country about one million years ago. A deep-freeze climate seized the ice fields to the north and great storms dumped tons of snow on the ice. It piled miles high, creating enormous pressure on the ice beneath. Eventually, it forced the glacier outward, and the entire ice flow began a sluggish journey to the south.

The advancing ice mountains, some two hundred feet high and three hundred miles wide, bulldozed along at twelve feet per day. They crushed everything in their path as far west as Kansas and Nebraska and as far south as the Ohio River. As they pressed into the Great Lakes region, their enormous weight chiseled great gorges into the earth. The frozen mountains stuffed these holes with ice.

Then the warming period came, and the ice reached the southern border of its coverage. Here it began to melt and the glacier line retreated toward the north. But the ice in the gorges stayed behind; it was lower, therefore colder, than the ice above it in the main flow. When it eventually did melt, the gorges and water formed the first crude Great Lakes.

The ice retreated to a point of equilibrium between the hot sun and freezing cold. Here the melting stopped, the pressure of the snow built up and once again the ice flow resumed its southward trek. Within a mere thousand years, the ice returned to torture the land until the next warming period sent it north again.

The whole cycle was repeated; there were probably four, possibly five, of these ice ages in the past million years. Each time, the newly formed lakes refroze and picked up more ice. The fresh ice heaps continually enlarged and reshaped the lake basins and surrounding terrain.

It was once believed that the back-and-forth pressure of the ice was the sole cause of the lakes' beginnings. But recent evidence indicates that an ancient system of rivers pre-dated the ice ages. Situated in wide, shallow valleys, these rivers and their branches drained either into the Hudson Bay area or the St. Lawrence Valley. According to this

modern theory, when the ice finally plowed its way through the terrain, it obstructed these drainage areas. So the rivers could no longer flow and they backed up into their shallow valleys. This helped the ice in its formation of the lakes.

When the lakes were crammed with ice, the pressure began to split their deep gorges in many places. As the ice melted in each warming period, these fissures and their adjacent terrain became rivers. Some were independent while others formed new waterways connecting with the pre-glacial river beds.

As the melting continued, the overflowing lakes needed still more escape routes. They spilled into each other, forming a linked group. However, an ice wall cut off the water's escape through the St. Lawrence area. So it burst free in other areas, forming the beginnings of such rivers as the Chicago, the Wabash and the Grand. When the St. Lawrence ice wall finally melted, escape streams to the Atlantic were formed. These became rivers like the Mohawk, the Hudson and the Ottawa.

The advancing ice mountains pushed rivers of rock before them. They carved off peaks of hills, mixing together top soils, crushed rocks and minerals. Part of this load was ground below the lake bottoms by the weight of the ice. During warming periods, part of this till that was amassed in the ice dropped to form the lake bottoms. The rest of the rich mixture was spread over the surrounding land, creating one of the world's richest agricultural heartlands.

About ten thousand years ago, the final ice sheets began to recede. Lake Erie was the first Great Lake to emerge in approximately its present state; it made its debut several thousand years before Babylon became a great city in 2,000 B.C. Lake Michigan was next to be freed. Both lakes were nearly complete before the glaciers released their icy grip on the others. Lake Ontario appeared about six thousand years ago and lakes Huron and Superior were liberated within the past five thousand years.

As the ice sheets receded for the last time, animal and plant life came to the Great Lakes. Fossilized whale remains have been located in the area around Lake Huron where a gigantic arm once cut through from the ocean. Mastodons and musk oxen foraged the land. They inhabited the region until the first people, forerunners of the American Indians, gradually drove them out.

This, then, is how the Great Lakes began. To the harsh influx of rock and ice, they owe their enormous wealth and rugged beauty. In this rich and lovely state, they greeted the arrival of man.

Ontario Ministry of Industry and Tourism

The rocky coast of Tobermory, at the tip of Lake Huron's Bruce Peninsula, is part of the hard limestone of the Niagara Escarpment which arcs across the Great Lakes from Niagara Falls to Wisconsin's Door County.

Overleaf: *Endless wind and waves have carved the enormous cliffs of the Minnesota shore. This is part of the Canadian Shield, among the oldest rock on earth.*

Ken Dequaine

Warriors, Missionaries and Redcoats

When the first people, the American Indians, arrived, it was with a great love for the lakes around them. Here lived their gods, in the mysterious islands of Lake Superior, in the changing seasons of Lake Ontario. The Indians were deeply religious nature worshippers; the good spirits brought them harvest, the bad brought blight.

For thousands of years Indian nations migrated into the Great Lakes region, settling there to enjoy the endless supply of black bass, whitefish and delicious trout. The lakes were easy routes to their hunting grounds by bark canoes, but they were also easy tracks to war. And so they fought. A succession of tribes decimated and dispossessed their forerunners over and over again for hundreds of years.

Scores of tribes settled in the region, but none were more integrally involved in the Great Lakes' story than the mighty nations of the Iroquois.

The Iroquois came from the west, pushing into the Lake Ontario surroundings. Eventually they would become a terrifying foe to the rest of the native tribes. But at first the Iroquois coexisted with their neighbors. The Huron and the Iroquois nations were of the same linguistic stock and racial stock; they could understand each other's language. During their migration, the Huron split to the north, settling south of Georgian Bay. The Neutral (believed to be the parent tribe of all Huron-Iroquois peoples) moved to the south and east of the Huron. Two great Iroquois tribes, the

(continued on page 17)

The huts of the Chippewa encampment in Sault Ste. Marie, *an 1846 oil painting by Canadian Paul Kane, were made by stretching birch bark over limber saplings. In the background is the St. Mary's River.*

Royal Ontario Museum, Toronto

An artist's impression, this drawing depicts the rocky wilderness of
Lake Superior's north shore before the white man extensively settled it.

Mohawk and Onondaga, claimed territory to the east of Lake Ontario while several other Iroquois tribes moved to the south of it. This was all hundreds of years before the first white men interrupted Indian lives.

The Iroquois built their long, bark-sided houses inland from the shore. Every ten years or so, when the firewood grew scarce and the soil became less fertile, they would simply pack up and move to a place where the grass was greener. They were a Stone Age culture with simple hammers and hoes; not until whites arrived were their tomahawks made of iron.

The women raised corn and beans, squash and pumpkins; human flesh was eaten only when other supplies ran low. Agriculture was left to the women and old men. Young warriors far preferred the thrills, the excitement of war.

Through wars, they extended their rule in every direction. Only intervention of the white man prevented the Iroquois from conquering everything east of the Mississippi.

The accomplishments of their warriors were backed by political strength. No other tribe could match them for organization. In the middle 1500's, five nations of the Iroquois banded together into the League, or Confederacy, of the Long House. The five nations involved were the Mohawk, Onondaga, Oneida, Cayuga and Seneca. They would protect each other from hostile tribes and promote each other's interests. All other tribes, even Iroquois groups that refused to join, became the enemy. The Iroquois Confederacy was so politically sound that it even impressed a nation-builder like Benjamin Franklin.

At their peak, the Iroquois never numbered over fifteen thousand and of these, only five thousand were members of the League. Yet their Confederacy made them the greatest of conquerors. Its strength held out for nearly two centuries until the constant pull between the French and British finally broke the Iroquois down. But its effect on the early white settlers forms a major chapter in the Great Lakes' story.

The Iroquois were the strongest of the lake Indians but probably the Chippewa, or Ojibway, were the most numerous. Around twenty-five thousand claimed the lands that drained into Lake Superior and northern Lake Huron.

The Chippewa were nomads who cared little for the planting and reaping of crops; far better were the wildlife of their vast forests and the whitefish of their cold upper lakes. Each band of Chippewa, consisting of several family groups, claimed a spacious territory and in turn, each family group was responsible for hunting a set portion of the territory.

The organization of the Chippewa was not as defined as that of the Iroquois. Each band had a leader but no governing body united all of the bands. Because a man could not marry a woman of his same group, the bands did become quite interrelated. So kinship, as well as their language, became the major cohesive bonds.

Due to their frequent moves, the Chippewa invented an early variety of mobile home. They carried with them wide strips of birch bark, sewn to twenty-foot lengths. These were thrown over frames, rapidly constructed of limber saplings. With each move, the women simply rolled up the birch strips and toted them along.

Very few Chippewa bands stayed put long enough to plant crops. For vegetables, they traded with agricultural tribes or depended on what wild rice and berries they could find. In the spring, they harvested sap in birchbark buckets to make maple sugar.

The Chippewa religion was based on the mixture of good and evil forces that competed for the world. Most of the delightful legends that pervade the upper lakes are stories from the imaginative Chippewa. Several are told in later chapters.

While the lower lakes were dominated by the Iroquois, and the Chippewa generally ran the Superior show, Lake Michigan was possessed by several major tribes. Foremost were the Winnebago who for centuries had farmed northeast Wisconsin, in the vicinity of the lower Door Peninsula and Green Bay. Expert agriculturists, they raised bountiful crops of squash, corn and tobacco. Their homes were dome-shaped wigwams, topped with woven mats.

The Winnebago were strictly organized into clans. Some of these were superior to others. Those on the top, like the Thunderbird and Bear clans, shared governmental duties.

Socially and politically similar to the Winnebago were their northern neighbors, the Sauk and the Menominee. The Sauk grew crops by summer and hunted the buffalo to the west by winter. The Menominee planted few crops but depended on the abundance of wild rice in their lands. As they harvested the rice, they would drop part of the seeds into the water, automatically planting the crop for the following year. The Winnebago, Sauk and Menominee were all excellent weavers, fashioning sturdy material from vegetable fibers and buffalo hair.

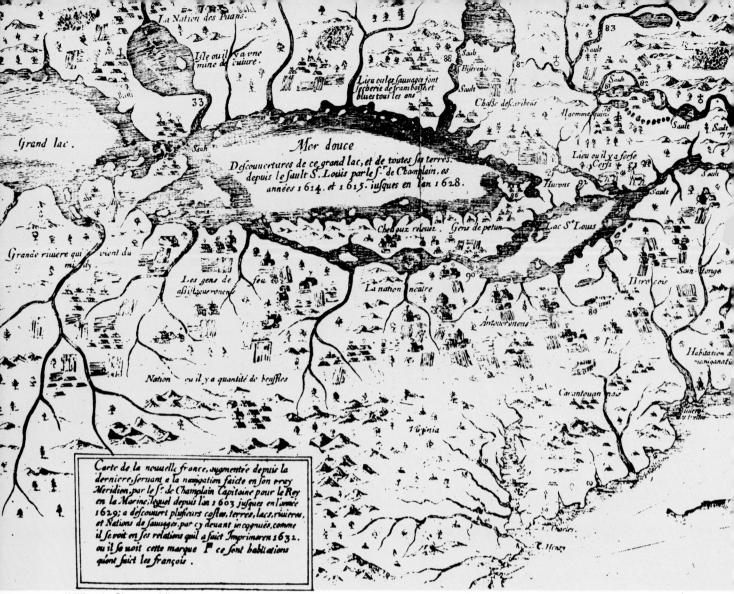

The largest tribe to the south of the Winnebago was the Miami. Bands of this tribe ringed Lake Michigan from southeast Wisconsin to southwest Michigan. Like the Sauk, they lived in permanent villages, leaving only for the winter buffalo hunt. They would ignite the prairie grass around a herd, leaving only a short arc of the circle free from flames. Here, as the buffalo stampeded through, they were felled by bow and arrow. As many as two hundred died in one day. The meat was dried and would last the Miami for many months.

Like the Winnebago, the Miami lived in dome-shaped wigwams. Their villages were frequently fortified with stockades. Their ships were dugout canoes; birchbark crafts were foreign to the Miami.

Several tribes shared southern Lake Michigan with the Miami. Most notable were the Potawatomi who dominated the Chicago area and southern Michigan. They were culturally similar to the Ottawa, farther north in Michigan's Lower Peninsula.

Both tribes cared less for agriculture than did most Lake Michigan dwellers. What farming they did was less extensive; more emphasis was placed on wild harvests of nuts, roots and berries. They lived by deer, elk and bear, using the fur and skin as clothing. Fish augmented game as the major food source.

Like the Chippewa, Ottawa bands held their own territories and were politically independent of each other. But, also like the Chippewa, strong kinship ties united the bands even though an overseeing government was missing.

These are just a few of the Great Lakes' tribes as they existed before Europeans arrived. While the Iroquois were leery of the whites, many tribes openly accepted them. In the following years the fur trade changed their culture from farming to hunting and miners dug holes in their ground and loggers stripped their forests. The tribes were buffeted and pushed around the lakes as white men saw fit. But the descendants of almost every tribe

Samuel de Champlain published this map of New France (opposite) before
lakes Erie or Michigan were discovered. The others hold roughly accurate positions.
Within palisades of stripped branches, Hurons built long, bark-sided houses. This one (above)
is in a replica of a seventeenth-century Huron village in Midland, Ontario.

can still be found in Great Lakes country today.

The first Frenchman to venture into the Canadian interior was Jacques Cartier. In 1535, he sailed his three little ships up the mighty St. Lawrence River to the site of present-day Montreal. But it was still over half a century before the first Great Lake was seen.

Samuel de Champlain was the first visitor recorded as reaching Lake Huron. Like all the early explorers, he had hoped to reach the Orient. In fact, when he established Quebec in 1608, it was as an advanced station on the route to the Indies.

In Quebec he heard stories from the Indians who came to trade their furs. They spoke of *La Mer Douce*, the sweetwater lake. In 1615, Champlain started out to locate this Western sea. With him went a scruffy young interpreter, Etienne Brulé,

and a gray-robed Récollet priest, Father Joseph Le Caron, who would stay in New France saving Huron souls until Quebec fell to the British in 1629.

On his expedition, Champlain took the route that would become the main thoroughfare to the west for missionaries, explorers and fur traders. He journeyed up the Ottawa River through back-breaking portages, fleets of mosquitoes and tree-tangled wilderness. His little party of canoes entered Lake Nipissing, paddled down the French River and emerged on Georgian Bay in July 1615. Champlain was unaware of the immensity of Lake Huron just beyond him, but he was sure Cathay lay on the opposite shore.

Champlain is given credit for recording this first sighting but it is believed that Le Caron, in an

Frances A. Hopkins accompanied her husband, a member of the Hudson's Bay Company, into the Northern wilderness. She recorded her journey in oil paintings of voyageurs and their canoes. In Canoes in a Fog: Lake Superior, 1869, she pictured herself in the closest canoe.

advance party, saw it a few days earlier. It is almost certain Brulé had seen it years before because he had roamed this country since 1610. He had lived with the Indians, becoming almost one with them.

Brulé preceded Champlain on their southward journey; Champlain sent him ahead on a mission to find the headwaters of the Susquehanna River. To do this, he must have crossed Lake Ontario, so he is credited with its first sighting. Champlain arrived at the sand dunes of Quinte on Lake Ontario later in 1615.

Brulé also was the first to view Lake Superior; in 1622, he saw where ancestors of the Chippewa took copper from the northern lake's shore. And he traveled through the lands of the Neutral Indians in 1624 so he could easily have stumbled onto Lake Erie. Brulé may have been the first white man to see every Great Lake except Michigan. But the illiterate young adventurer left no record. So what he saw and knew are now mysteries. In 1632, he died in a drunken brawl in Huron country and was eaten by his Indian associates.

In 1627, the British blockaded Quebec and took Champlain as a prisoner. He lived in England for five years before returning to Canada as governor. For three years he worked to build his beloved colony by promoting immigration, the fur trade, and making maps and records. Then on Christmas night in 1635, he died in Quebec. To him rightly goes the title, Father of New France.

The many French missionaries who came to New France to save the souls of their red children did as much to open the wilderness as did the explorers. The Récollets came first, then the Jesuits and Sulpicians. As a group, they were a brave, self-sacrificing lot, constantly threatened by Indian wars. They are remembered not only for the work they did at the time, but for their gifts to posterity. Almost all the records we have of this era are the writings of these early priests.

Throughout the settlement of Canada, the French had great difficulties living with the Iroquois Confederacy. There were several reasons. Champlain, through a serious error in judgment, alienated the Mohawk almost before exploration began. Also, the incoming French befriended the Huron. This was logical because the Huron were their closest neighbors. But they were also Iroquois enemies. Finally, the Iroquois were jealous of any other tribe who traded with the French.

The results of all this were Iroquois raids into Huron country, and the result of that was grave danger to the missionaries there (the Huron loved the gentle fathers but the Iroquois were never

*In 1673 Father Jacques Marquette and Louis Joliet explored
Lake Michigan and the Mississippi River Valley — Marquette
to teach Christianity to the Indians, Joliet to claim lands for France.*
Marquette and the Indians, 1673, *by Wilhelm Lamprecht.*

impressed with the strange Bible stories). So the Jesuits built a stone fort named Ste. Marie in 1634 for their own protection. One missionary, Jean de Brébeuf, was caught outside the fort by an Iroquois raiding party. He was tortured until he died, but his unflinching bravery so impressed the Iroquois chief that he ate the missionary's heart. Fort Ste. Marie has been restored and still stands today near Midland, Ontario.

Indian wars remained a constant problem for the French. In 1634, Champlain sent Jean Nicolet to restore the peace between the Huron and a Western tribe the Huron referred to as "People of the Stinking Water." While he was at it, Nicolet was to bring back information on fur trade possibilities as well as to look for a route to the Orient. So he took along a multi-colored robe of Chinese dam-

ask, embroidered with birds and flowers, to wear when he met the Oriental monarch.

Nicolet set out from Quebec up the familiar Ottawa route to the west. Six Huron paddled his single canoe. They subsisted on boiled Indian corn for the long journey past Manitoulin Island, through Le Cheneaux Islands (here Nicolet may have ventured up into Lake Superior). Passing the Straits of Mackinac, he encountered Lake Michigan — the first white man to do so.

As Nicolet approached the peninsula of Green Bay, he excitedly donned his flashy robe and fired off two pistols. The half-naked Winnebago who lined the shore to stare at him were astounded by the "Great Spirit" man with thunder in his hands.

The great feast of 120 beaver that the Winnebago offered Nicolet may have helped soothe his chagrin at having missed the Orient. But Nicolet's journey was not a total failure: He got the Indian peace treaty, he worked out plans for an increased fur trade, and he discovered one of the greatest lakes in the world.

Northern Lake Huron was no mystery after Nicolet's journey. In the fall of 1641, Father Isaac Jogues and Father Charles Raymbault further explored it on their way to Sault Ste. Marie. Here they learned of another Indian band, the Sioux, residing at the west end of Lake Superior. This small band was an eastern extension of the mighty plains tribe to the west. Some time later, a trade route to the Sioux for their buffalo robes was established. A year after this journey, Jogues was tortured and killed by Mohawk warriors.

All these Iroquois raids led up to the French and Indian War of 1643. The Iroquois pushed into Huron country with two objectives: to win this prized beaver land and to exterminate the Huron. The Iroquois had received guns in trade with the Dutch settlers in New York and Albany and the agricultural Huron were no match for them. Most were destroyed by the 1650's. The few remaining escaped along the southern shore of Lake Superior to its west end.

So by 1650, the French fur trade was at a standstill. It was much too dangerous to transport the furs from the west down to Quebec and Montreal through the ravaged Huron lands. This was a panicky situation for New France; its only revenue was from the furs.

A very few traders did manage to get through. Two notable explorer/traders were Ménard Chouart, sieur des Groseilliers, and his brother-in-law, Pierre Esprit Radisson. They were the first to record a journey to the west end of Lake Superior. Radisson was delighted with the rugged wilderness and with the plentiful "staggs, buffs, elands and castors [deer, buffalo, elk and beaver]." They returned from their two-thousand-mile journey in 1660 with a tremendous canoe train of furs.

But fur trading remained slow and sporadic as the Iroquois continued their marauding. Finally, in 1666, Louis XIV sent French troops to New France to halt the Iroquois. Following a treaty in 1667, the Iroquois remained more or less quiet for twenty years. This peace made settlers secure once again. It also afforded a safe base from which exploration could begin once more.

(continued on page 26)

Overleaf: *When the cannon fire ceased, Oliver Hazard Perry had decisively defeated the British fleet on September 10, 1813. Thomas Birch recaptured the burning brigs and billowing sails in his oil painting,* The Battle of Lake Erie.
From Pennsylvania Academy of the Fine Arts

For over two centuries, fur posts were sprinkled around the upper lakes. Typically, they were built where missions had already begun a settlement. Indian villages grew up beside them to be close to the trading. This post was at Fond du Lac, Wisconsin.

Minnesota Historical Society

About this time, Father Claude Jean Allouez set out to search for the few Huron who had escaped the Iroquois wrath. He found them in a tiny village in Chequamegon Bay on Lake Superior, near today's Ashland, Wisconsin. Here he built a hut for himself and a chapel of bark. It was the first mission west of Lake Huron.

Jean Talon had become the intendant of New France in 1665. He was actively interested in exploration, mostly due to Indian tales of copper in the northern lake. In 1669 he sent Louis Joliet north to the Sault via the old Ottawa River route. Joliet was to take supplies to Jean Peré, a *coureur de bois* (woods runner or traveler) who was investigating Lake Superior copper mines. Joliet never located Peré, but he did free an Iroquois prisoner from the stake. This Indian told Joliet of an easier route back to Montreal. The Indian went with him to guide the way. Joliet paddled south from the St. Mary's River, descending Lake Huron to the St. Clair River. Here he passed through Lake St. Clair to the Detroit River. When he emerged from it, he was the first white man known to see Lake Erie.

Lake Erie had remained a mystery more than half a century after the founding of Lake Huron. Why was the lake discovered so late? There were three main reasons. First, the St. Lawrence River was in the land of the Iroquois Confederacy. Explorers could not take this logical route inland. Second, the old Ottawa River route took explorers far north of Lake Erie to Georgian Bay. And everyone knew China lay to the west, not the south. Finally, fur and copper also were in the west and north, drawing the traders away from the lower lake.

Joliet followed Lake Erie's north shore to the Grand River. Here he left the lake and went overland to a friendly Indian village at the head of Lake Ontario. In an odd coincidence for such a vast wilderness, Joliet met Robert Cavelier, sieur de La Salle, in this village. La Salle had pushed through the St. Lawrence (open after the Iroquois peace treaty) to explore the unknown west. He was less than pleased to meet the man who had beaten him to it. It is known that La Salle did not go on to Lake Erie, but just what he did do for the next few years is now lost to history. Joliet, shortly after his Lake Erie venture, began his famous expedition with Father Jacques Marquette.

Father Marquette had taken over the Allouez mission at Chequamegon Bay in the late 1660's. There he heard the Indian rumors of a great *Messi-Sipi* river. Marquette desperately wanted to search for this river. He prayed for permission to

do so. But in 1671, his Huron and Ottawa charges became involved in a battle with the Sioux. So the Indians and Marquette evacuated to the east to avoid certain destruction.

They ended their flight at St. Ignace, at the Straits of Mackinac, where the Indians built new villages and Marquette a new mission. He must have suffered tremendous disappointment because exploration of the Mississippi River now seemed a lost dream.

And then, along came Joliet, paddling up to Marquette's mission in December of 1672. He bore joyful news: He was commissioned to find the great river and Marquette's superiors had granted him permission to go along.

They made a fine pair, these two adventurers. Joliet was an experienced explorer and trained cartographer; Marquette knew all there was to know about the languages and country of Illinois. They started in May 1673 to locate the river and follow it to either the Gulf of Mexico or California — its destination was unknown.

With two bark canoes, five French *voyageurs* to handle the canoes, and a supply of smoked meat and Indian corn, the explorers crossed Lake Michigan to the Fox-Wisconsin waterway. On June 17, they arrived at the mile-wide Mississippi where it flowed along between towering cliffs. The little party followed the river for many days until its southward trend assured them that it went to the Gulf of Mexico. Near the Arkansas River they turned back, fearing they would be captured by the Spaniards if they continued.

Joliet rushed ahead, returning to Montreal with his news of the river in 1674. Marquette, with an illness from his journey, lagged behind. The sickness stayed with him, and he died near Ludington, Michigan, on the return journey to his mission. Two years later, the Indians exhumed his body and cleaned the bones in their old tribal custom. The bones they carried to St. Ignace and buried beneath the mission. In 1877 the long-forgotten grave was rediscovered and most of the bones were given to Marquette University in Milwaukee.

Shortly before this Mississippi expedition, Louis de Baude, count de Palluau et de Frontenac, became the power in New France. He had been ordered to keep the Iroquois in line, develop more trade, and encourage marriage of "youths at twenty years and girls at fifteen." Underpopulation was a chronic problem for the Canadian wilderness.

To accomplish the first objective, Frontenac ordered a fort built on Lake Ontario. At this point La Salle's story comes to light again because it was he who built and commanded Fort Frontenac. He

Breaking ice allowed these schooners to leave Duluth in 1875. About
1,700 schooners sailed the Great Lakes at this time but their demise was imminent
as steamers chugged into view; the last lake schooner was built in 1889.

also constructed two small sailing vessels, the first on the Great Lakes. These conveyed furs and supplies between Fort Frontenac at one end of the lake and Niagara at the other. They also reminded the Iroquois and the British, who wished to push into the rich fur trade, that the French were watching.

La Salle's goal, however, was not to end his career as a fort's commander. He had a dream of a fabulous French empire. He wished to go to the Mississippi, establish a colony, and follow the river to its mouth at the Gulf. There he would claim it for France. That would cut the Spanish claim in two, and most important, it would fence in the British on the Atlantic Coast.

To accomplish this dream, La Salle would need a ship to carry supplies to his colony and return with furs to pay for the goods. This ship must be built on Lake Erie, because a ship on Ontario could not cross the thundering falls of Niagara. Thus, in 1678, La Salle sent a party of thirty men with

shipbuilding supplies to the other side of the falls. There on the Niagara River, where Cayuga Creek emptied into it, the men constructed the forty-five-ton *Griffin*. Under the watchful eyes of wary Indians, the little ship took shape. It had a griffin on its prow and an eagle on its high stern. Two tall masts held the square sails, and the ship displayed five new cannons.

La Salle joined his party when the *Griffin* was ready to sail in August 1679. The current of the upper Niagara proved too much for the little craft so a dozen men on land towed it onto Lake Erie. With the boastful, vagabond priest, Father Louis Hennepin, and a highly skeptical crew, La Salle sailed on his way toward his dream.

The *Griffin* finally arrived at Washington Island off the tip of the Door Peninsula. It was late in the season, so La Salle had it immediately loaded with furs and sent on its homeward journey. La Salle, Hennepin and a small party pushed on by canoe to the mouth of the St. Joseph

27

River. Shortly after the *Griffin* set sail, a violent four-day storm racked Lake Michigan, and the gallant little craft was never seen again. The Great Lakes had claimed their first ship.

The *Griffin* had been scheduled to meet La Salle with fresh supplies. When it did not arrive, he returned overland to Fort Frontenac to make new arrangements for the goods he needed. It was not until 1682 that La Salle finally arrived at the Mississippi. Two months later, he reached its mouth. There, in a great pompous ceremony, he claimed all the country drained by the river and its tributaries for the King of France.

This was the last of the famous expeditions for Great Lakes' explorers. For the next several decades, the history of the Great Lakes was a bloody procession of wars involving the Indians, French, British and Americans. Between 1690 and 1748 three wars were fought between the French and the English. These were primarily European struggles; strife in the New World was only a side show.

The most notable occurrence during these wartorn years was the construction of Fort Pontchartrain at Detroit. Antoine de la Mothe Cadillac constructed the fort in 1701 as a safeguard against British invasion of the upper lakes. It was at this fort that the French began the lengthy Fox War.

The French believed that the arrogant, high-spirited Fox tribe was getting too friendly with the British. So, with French backing, the other tribes around Detroit descended on the surprised Fox, slaughtering the warriors, torturing the women and children. The few Fox survivors waged a terrible war against the French and their allies for many years to come. In return, the French pledged themselves to destroy all of the Fox. The tribe eventually dwindled in number so that only a few tattered remains finally fled into eastern Iowa. There the French abandoned the war.

The Great Lakes and the St. Lawrence and Mississippi rivers were now all possessions of New France. The British, along the Atlantic seaboard, had believed their New World claims extended all the way to the Pacific Ocean. Therefore, the two empires clashed over who actually owned what. To add to the problem, the French were antagonized by the British who steadily moved in on the valuable fur trade, and they believed the English were turning the Indians against them by promising the natives better trade deals.

These harsh feelings exploded into the Seven Years' War in 1756. The French were severely outmanned and had only wit to match the British strength. They fought well, but Montreal fell in 1760. The frightened French governor surrendered all of Canada even though the war to the west was still undecided. The war was officially ended in the Treaty of Paris three years later. New France was no more.

British domination over the Great Lakes was a short, explosive affair. But the years were financially lucrative; the Lake Superior fur trade reached its peak under English rule.

No sooner had the British taken possession of the land than they began having Indian problems. The Indians, lead by the great Ottawa chief, Pontiac, resented the English for claiming land that the Indians had never ceded to the French. The British didn't understand or like the Indians; many thought the natives were no better than the rest of the woodland animals. Pontiac watched with growing concern the influx of British settlers. The result of these tensions was a short but bloody war in 1763. Pontiac led a siege of Detroit and many settlers died before Pontiac's Rebellion was quelled.

During the Revolutionary War, the Americans took Detroit and Niagara. The British kept them out of the rest of the Great Lakes due in part to their naval power and in part to the Americans' short supplies. But raw feelings built up between the former countrymen. The Americans wanted the British to leave land that Americans thought was theirs and they wanted to take over the rich fur trade. The British chose not to give up the land and backed the Indians in vicious strikes against the American settlers. Both sides moved reluctantly into the War of 1812.

This war is notable primarily for the amazing blunders on both sides. The Americans thought it would be an easy win; instead, the new country suffered many humiliating defeats. Only one victory in the Great Lakes area stands out. It was one of the few American victories, but a decisive one.

The Americans realized they could not win the war without a fleet on the Great Lakes to destroy the English ships. Commodore Oliver Hazard Perry was given the ominous chore of creating such a fleet. He had to build ten ships on Lake Erie which was under British control.

Construction began in two small shipyards. Black Rock, New York, was to build five ships and Erie was to prepare two brigs and three schooners. The British guns of Fort Erie hampered construction of the Black Rock ships. In a battle that was imperative to win, the Americans knocked out this English fort.

When the ships were finally ready, the Black Rock fleet moved to Erie to join forces. Just why the English allowed these ships to be built and why they made no effort to keep the two fleets from merging are mysteries of the war.

Perry chose one of the Erie brigs, the *Lawrence*, as his flagship. Both it and the *Niagara* were handsome ships. Their keels were of finely crafted black oak; their iron work had been scrounged from wherever the shipbuilders could find it. The bold, adventurous Perry instilled in his reluctant sailors a bravado that equaled his own. In August 1813, the little fleet sailed out to find Captain R. H. Barclay, commander of the British fleet. At Sandusky, Perry picked up one hundred sharp-shooters whose skills he would need when the fleets met in close combat.

Perry chose the waters near Put-in-Bay in the Erie Islands as the place to blockade Fort Malden and force out the British fleet. There he waited until September 10, 1813, when six English ships sailed out to battle. The troops at Malden had run out of food; Barclay had to break the blockade.

The wind was light; slowly the fleets approached each other. The British with their long guns opened fire first, hitting Perry's flagship. In a few hours the little brig was destroyed. Perry and a handful of sailors took the only boat on the *Lawrence* that was not destroyed and rowed across to the *Niagara*. This brig under Perry then moved in on Barclay's flagship and began a merciless broadside bombardment. All the officers on board the flagship were either wounded or dead by the time the British fleet finally surrendered. Perry officially accepted the surrender from the broken quarterdeck of the wrecked *Lawrence*. He scribbled a note on the back of an envelope to send to General William Henry Harrison: "We have met the enemy and they are ours."

After the Battle of Erie, the war soon closed. It ended formally on December 24, 1814, settling the border dispute between Canada and the United States. Three years later the Rush-Bagot agreement forever outlawed war on the Great Lakes. That was over one and a half centuries ago. So far, the treaty has worked.

As richer industries grew, many residents turned away from the rugged life as fishermen. Their abandoned homes became mute testimony of the past.

Michigan Department of Natural Resources

Lakes of Plenty

Since the first Indian landed the first fat fish, the Great Lakes have been a rich resource for man. Placid, reedy river mouths blossomed to busy harbors; isolated missions swelled to bustling cities. Where traffic to and from Lake Superior was once blocked by the St. Mary's River rapids, today more cargo is hauled annually than through the Suez and Panama canals combined. The states and province that border the Great Lakes form the largest industrial complex in the world.

The fur trade was the first treasure to draw the white man to the lakes. The European beaver stock had waned by 1600 so New World furs were a welcome savior for the desperate garment guilds. Marten, muskrat, otter and fox all donated their pelts so fashionable society could have fur on its back. However, beaver was king of the trade. These industrious dam-builders ranged throughout Canada and the northern United States in a seemingly endless supply. A few that were skinned were also consumed; the French regarded them as aquatic animals similar to mackerels. Hence, they could be eaten on "meager" days. Eventually so many died in the traders' traps that they were nearly exterminated around the Great Lakes.

Indians often hunted by night, felling the beaver with arrows. An incessant fund of snares, pits and iron traps awaited the beaver wherever he roamed the forest and built his ponds.

Traders passed from tribe to tribe gathering pelts that the Indians prepared. These traders frequently took wives in several tribes — it assured them friendly welcomes as they entered the villages to barter. Other whites invaded the Indian territory in groups to harvest their own furs.

The first of the great fur companies was British due to a French error. Groseilliers and Radisson had returned from the Lake Superior wilderness with a huge brigade of fur-laden canoes in 1660. They told the French officials the best beaver lands lay to the north and west of Lake Superior. The best route to it was through Hudson Bay.

(continued on page 33)

U. S. Fish and Wildlife Service

One of the Great Lakes' finest gifts is their many wildlife preserves.
Thousands of Canada geese nest here; others use the lakes as a rest area
on their migrations between their winter home, the Southern states,
and their summer place, the wind-riddled Arctic tundra.

*Many of the old portages used by eighteenth-
century fur traders are still open to modern-day voyageurs.
The Boundary Waters Canoe Area in Minnesota and Ontario
offers a wealth of waters for ideal canoeing.*

Les Blacklock

The French ignored their story, so Groseilliers and Radisson told the British. The English, eagerly seeking any inroad to the fur trade, listened, and this led to the founding of the fantastically rich Hudson's Bay Company.

Groseilliers and Radisson were right; it was an easier trip to the beaver stores through the bay than the lakes. From then on, the French traders around Lake Superior had serious problems competing with the British to the north.

In the 1670's, Grand Portage, on the west end of Lake Superior, became the chief jumping-off point to the northwest beaver country. It was Minnesota's first settlement; there the traders from the Northwest would meet the *voyageurs* from Montreal to exchange their furs for trade goods.

The *voyageurs* were hardy men, although barely five feet tall and 150 pounds. Ten to fifteen of them were the "motors" for the large *maître*, or Montreal canoes. These canoes were birchbark sewn with roots over white cedar ribs. They carried several tons of cargo (muskets, knives, blankets and rum on the way to Grand Portage and fur on the way back) plus a mast and sail. The fur or supplies were tied into ninety-pound bundles. Each *voyageur* carried at least two bundles over the thirty-six portages from Montreal to Grand Portage. For two cents an hour, they paddled sixteen to eighteen hours a day, seven days a week, averaging at least fifty miles a day. They stopped twice each day to dine on a boiled concoction of salt pork, dried peas and corn. Through it all they remained cheerful, docile and courteous. The *voyageurs* were known for the many songs they sang while paddling along the shore, and for the bright colored sashes, yards long, wound around their waists. More than any other group, the *voyageurs* are responsible for opening the lakes country.

Each spring the *voyageurs* arrived at Grand Portage to meet the North men, traders who paddled out of the interior to trade their year's supply of pelts. Their smaller North canoes were manned by six to ten paddlers and carried a three-thousand-pound cargo. At Grand Portage, over a thousand North men and *voyageurs* would mingle, smoking their tiny clay pipes, roughhousing, dancing with Indian girls in the Great Hall to bagpipe and fiddle tunes. They would spend the nights sleeping under their overturned canoes and after their trading was complete, return to the north or Montreal.

The French did the groundwork for the fur trade, but it reached its peak under British rule. In 1784, the next great trading company was founded. A hodgepodge of traders, *voyageurs* and

Olive Glasgow

A beaver lodge is a five-foot-high rounded heap of interlaced branches and leaves which can be entered only through underwater passageways. After the winter freeze, the beavers within the snug chamber have almost impenetrable protection.

interpreters began the North West Company to curtail the growing rivalries between each other. They hoped to present a united front against the ever growing powerhouse, the Hudson's Bay Company. They did quite well for several years, establishing stockaded posts all over Lake Superior. They even opened a sawmill at Sault Ste. Marie to supply lumber for their forts. But because they were such a mottled group, their organization eventually broke down. Two separate factions splintered away from them leaving the main company weak, and it was finally sold to Hudson's Bay Company in 1821.

Hudson's Bay would probably have become the undisputed fur king if it were not for a New Yorker named John Jacob Astor. He began his American Fur Company in 1808 and by 1816 had convinced Congress to block all foreign trade in American territory. Thus the British were banned from lower Lake Superior.

Astor sold a large bulk of his furs in China. With the proceeds he purchased tea and silk which he then sold in Europe. There he bought industrial goods to sell in the fast-growing American market. With the funds from this he made the final transaction, Astor bought Manhattan real estate.

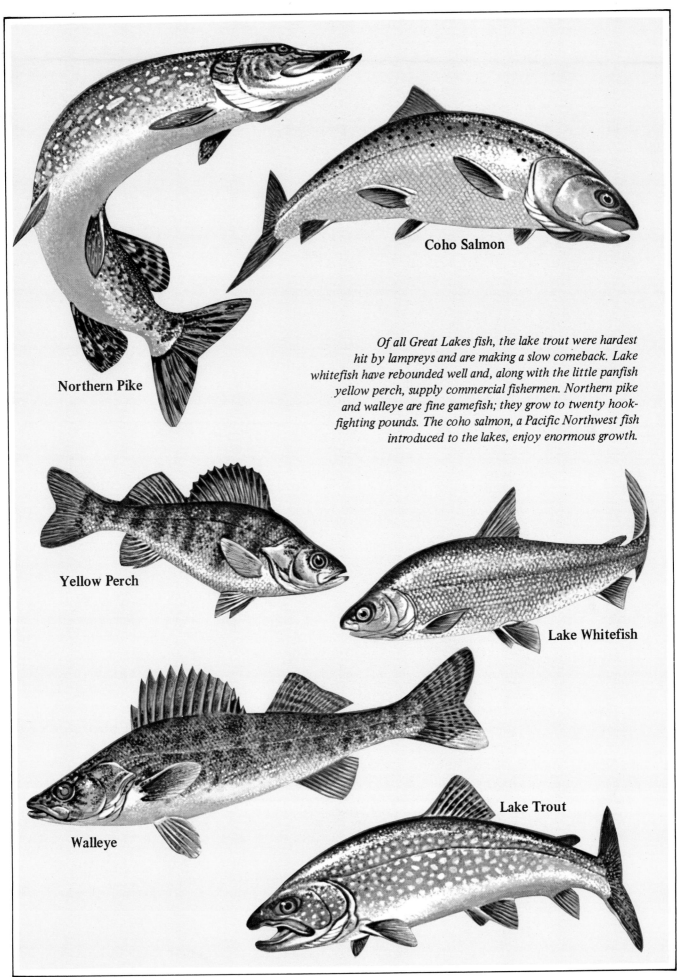

Coho Salmon

Northern Pike

Of all Great Lakes fish, the lake trout were hardest hit by lampreys and are making a slow comeback. Lake whitefish have rebounded well and, along with the little panfish yellow perch, supply commercial fishermen. Northern pike and walleye are fine gamefish; they grow to twenty hook-fighting pounds. The coho salmon, a Pacific Northwest fish introduced to the lakes, enjoy enormous growth.

Yellow Perch

Lake Whitefish

Lake Trout

Walleye

Tom Algire

Astor not only knew how to get the most out of the fur trade, he knew when to get out of it completely. In 1833, he sold his interests; in 1848, the company went bankrupt. By the late 1850's, the fur trade was dead because the beaver were scarce and the clothing fashions had changed. But it was hardly noticed. By then a new treasure was tantalizing the Great Lakes' dwellers — copper.

The first metal mined in North America was probably on the Keweenaw point which thrusts into Lake Superior from Michigan's Upper Peninsula. Indians mined copper there thousands of years ago. They worshipped the *caignetdaze*, endowing it with mystical powers and wearing it in their medicine bags. They chipped chunks of copper away from the exposed veins. Then, with stone mallets, they hammered it into axes, knives and fish hooks. Remains of their ancient diggings can still be found in abundance on Isle Royale.

Rumors of copper pervaded the Great Lakes for decades. Champlain heard the stories when he founded Quebec in 1608. It allegedly lay strewn around the ground in lumps just waiting to be picked up. Both the French and British searched for it with very little success. It was not until Michigan became a state in 1837 that the true copper country was finally discovered.

Michigan had to give up the valuable "Toledo strip" to Ohio to gain its statehood. Congress offered it the Upper Peninsula as a consolation prize. Michigan grudgingly accepted the "worthless" wilds and decided to run down the copper rumor. The State's legislature hired Douglass Houghton as state geologist and shipped him off to the Upper Peninsula to look around. In his report of 1841, he confirmed that the rich resource did exist. But Houghton was not optimistic. He seemed worried that many adventurers would lose their shirts looking for it. But nobody listened. The first ore rush in America was under way.

By 1843 hundreds of farmers and settlers had turned prospector. They swarmed over the Keweenaw searching for ore. Some found chunks of metal on the ground and began digging right on the spot. But this was "float" copper; it had been torn away from the main lodes during the Ice Age and carried miles away. Other miners blasted away in the ancient Indian mine pits. They got a little copper that the Indians had been unable to chip

out, but it was a small return for their efforts. Ultimately, most miners called it quits and went home after spending everything they had. Houghton's worry about them proved well-founded.

In 1845, with the "get rich quick" adventurers out of the way, the organized mine companies moved in. The Pittsburgh and Boston Company opened the Cliff Mine south of Eagle River. It struggled along for three years; then new veins were opened and the company boomed. In the next thirty-five years it produced thirty-eight million pounds of copper.

Other efforts were quite successful in the Keweenaw's rock fissures. Then the huge Pewabic lode was discovered in a main lava flow. By 1862, its ores were boosting the Yankees toward victory in the Civil War.

For many years the Keweenaw led the world in copper production until the great Montana lodes took over. Today, most of the early mines stand empty, surrounded with their own debris.

Iron ore was the next great mining venture. It had been known for years that iron existed somewhere in the ground around the Great Lakes; there is evidence that Father Marquette had heard about it. But the copper craze had detracted from iron because it was not as pure as copper; it was mixed with useless stone. So its price per pound was less. Besides, early America just did not have the blast furnaces necessary to make it a useful product.

The location of the iron-ore veins was definitely established in 1844. A government surveyor, William A. Burt, could not make his compass work; the needle moved erratically instead of pointing to the North. It was being drawn to the heavy gray rocks around him. These were only half stone; the other half was iron ore.

Shortly thereafter, Phil M. Everett formed the Jackson Mining Company and headed north looking for copper or silver. He heard of Burt's discovery and hired a Chippewa chief, Marji-Gesick, to lead him to Burt's land of heavy rocks. The chief guided him to a spot on the Carp River, not far from present-day Marquette. There an outcropping of high-grade ore was exposed under an uprooted tree. Everett was disappointed that the gray ore was not silver or copper but he got together a crew and began operations in 1847. The Jackson mine never really showed a profit but it did begin one of the richest industries in history.

Throughout the second half of the nineteenth century miners searched the upper lakes for bigger and better iron ranges. Five more great ranges were

The moldering remains of defunct copper mines speckle Michigan's Keweenaw Peninsula. Descendants of the miners who worked the Central Mine until its demise in the 1890's hold an annual reunion among the ruins.

The lumber camp of the late 1800's was a mecca for any hardy adventurer who would tackle the Northern pine. The work was as hard as it was dangerous but the smell of enormous profit mingled with the sawdust in the air.

found to serve the growing number of blast furnaces in the lower lake cities.

The Mesabi, the biggest of all, was found in the Minnesota Arrowhead in 1892 by the Merritt brothers and nephews. *Mesabi* was an Indian word for "sleeping giant" and indeed it was. Billions of tons of high-grade ore, hematite, waited in the range. It was so rich the ore could just be blasted loose and scooped out. The mining companies joyfully bit into the ground, removing the metal at record rates. By the 1940's, the ore was in tremendous demand as America geared up its war effort. But at the same time, the high-grade ore was beginning to become depleted, and America started looking elsewhere for its war tools. Through the 50's and into the 60's, the upper Lake Superior country plunged into a deep economic depression. Thousands of miners had no more earth to tackle as one mine after another shut down.

The high-grade ore in the Mesabi was nearly gone. But it had been surrounded by an almost unlimited supply of taconite, a low-grade ore, with an iron content of only twenty-five to thirty percent, as compared to the fifty to sixty percent content of the hematite. This low-grade ore had

been overlooked because it was impractical to mine. But as the hematite gave out, the taconite looked much more attractive. The companies initiated research programs to find a way to convert it into a usable product. Their success was more than they hoped for. They found a way to make taconite even more attractive than the high-grade ore. Iron mining was saved.

One of the most picturesque eras in Great Lakes' history was the lumber boom that followed along just behind the mining exploitation.

The deep, green thickness of the lakeland forests distressed the early settlers; it had to be moved out before crops could move in. So they cut a bit for their firewood and barns, then chopped and burned away the rest to form clearings. But as the number of towns raised and ships being built increased, lumber became an asset.

Hence, the lumbering days began in the 1840's. Sawmills came to buzzing, screeching life in Saginaw Bay, Michigan. From there the loggers rushed north to Lake Superior and west to Lake Michigan, felling the tall dense forest that stood in their way.

On the mouth of nearly every sizable stream that rushed to the lakes, a sawmill was constructed.

From the inland logging camps, logs were floated downstream to the mills. Wooden "lumber hooker" ships carried the bounty from the mills to Chicago, Detroit, Milwaukee and every other thriving port.

Everybody became a logger. Farmers, storekeepers and immigrants from northern Europe joined the forest crews. The tents and grounds of the muddy logging camps swelled with loggers and horse teams. Huge cook shacks turned out sawdust-covered flapjacks for sawdust-covered lumberjacks. This was despite the fact that the fatality rate among loggers was enormous. If you were a cutter, you felled your tree and prayed that another cutter didn't fell his tree on top of you. If you were a top loader, you stacked the logs two stories high on sleds to be hauled to the river.

The lumber era began to come to an end. There was very little cutting after 1900 and by 1920 it had all stopped. There were two reasons: The best trees were gone and the great fires had begun.

As the loggers sliced through the forest they had left behind a trail of tree tops and branches. These dried to brittleness and in a hot, sere season, made fantastic kindling. By the 1870's enormous fires hit Wisconsin and Michigan. Hundreds of little blazes began, then joined together forming huge burning sheets. Time and again they swept the land, killing hundreds of people, destroying dozens of towns. Because forest fire-fighting methods were not developed until some years later, the incineration continued unchecked until enough rain could douse the blaze or until there was nothing left to burn. When the holocausts finally subsided, barren acres of charred stumps were all that remained of the mighty white pine. Then land erosion began as rainwater runoff clogged the streams with the once-rich topsoils.

At long last man began to help the land he had destroyed. The United States Forest Service began a program to reclaim the wounded country. By the 1930's, effective fire-fighting facilities were established. The Civilian Conservation Corps sent in crews to plant new trees. The little growth that had escaped the loggers and fires was nursed back to health. National forests were designated; today six of them cover immense tracts of lake country.

Primarily red and jack pines were planted in the reclaimed areas. Today, they are approaching or have reached lumbering size. The fast-growing aspen on burnt-over areas were once considered useless. They only made good nurse trees, reclaiming the ground until better trees could take root. But now the trees are valued for pulpwood and veneer. The new man-made forests are once again producing lumber but only under the principle of sustained yield — the amount cut does not exceed the amount grown.

Whalebacks, ancestors to modern lake freighters, were launched in the 1890's. Their flat snouts earned them the nickname "pig boats." In this old photograph, two whalebacks are docked in the icy Duluth harbor in 1893.

St. Louis County Historical Society

The forests have also provided new homes for Northern wildlife. Openings are created for the forest creatures and planted grasses sustain insects for game and songbirds. Beavers flourish again, as do deer, bears, foxes and weasels. The endangered sandhill crane spends a protected summer in these woods. Moose and timber wolves roam the Superior National Forest in northern Minnesota. And in the remote and lonely wilds, even the bald eagle is almost safe from man.

By the 1850's agriculture, mining and logging were all beginning to thrive. To support these new lifestyles, Great Lakes' shipping came into its own.

Lakes' shipping began with the earliest Indian canoes; until the Soo locks opened in 1855, canoes were still the dominant crafts. Most of these were birch bark, although in areas where the birch tree was scarce some were sided with elm. The bark was fitted to a wood frame, sewn with roots and sealed with pitch. Some of these crafts were large enough to carry fifty warriors to battle.

Following the canoe were schooners conveying lumber, steamers transporting immigrants and freighters laden with iron ore. But several obstacles sealed off the lakes from the outside world. So in order for this parade of ships to begin properly, canals had to be built.

The Erie Canal, finished in 1825, bridged the 363 miles between the Hudson River and Lake Erie. A series of canals circumvented the St. Lawrence River rapids connecting Lake Ontario with the Atlantic. The Welland Canal, opened in 1829, allowed the new Lake Ontario traffic to skirt Niagara Falls and enter Lake Erie. The backbreaking work of hauling ships on rollers through the streets of Sault Ste. Marie between lakes Huron and Superior ended when the first Soo locks finally joined the two Great Lakes. Lake Michigan was linked to the Mississippi River by the Illinois Waterway in 1848. These canals and locks joined with the lakes to create the greatest freshwater highway anywhere on earth.

In the early years of navigation, warships like the Niagara dotted the lakes. After the War of 1812, the passenger and freight business burgeoned. Shipyards up and down the Canadian and United States shores turned out steamers and sailing vessels of all description — square riggers, brigantines and schooners.

The first steamer on the lakes was a Canadian trader, the Frontenac, launched in 1816, and like all the early steamers, it carried sails to supplement its big churning paddle wheels. The sails were hoisted when the wind blew well to speed up the steamers economically. The Vandalia, launched in

Inland Steel Company

1841, was the first steamer with a screw propeller on the lakes. It set the trend that gradually made the picturesque paddle wheelers obsolete. The little ship could chug along at seven miles per hour or even faster when its sails caught a good wind.

By the 1850's well over one thousand steamers and schooners traveled the lakes. By the thousands, European immigrants left Buffalo by ship to settle the Northern lakes and farther west. The earliest passenger ships featured the crudest of accommodations. In a men's cabin and a women's cabin, bunks lined the walls on the inside of the hull. The sole luxury was a wood-burning stove in the center of each long cabin.

After the Civil War, the vacation trade grew and so did the luxury ships. Soon palatial vessels

The modern lake freighter is unmistakable with its superstructure fore and aft and a long, flat deck amidships. The largest freighter now on the lakes is longer than three football fields and can load over 57,000 tons. This ore ship is docked for the night at East Chicago, Indiana.

cruised from port to port. The era of majestic passenger ships ended only when the automobile and airplane took over.

Meanwhile lake freighters were developing in their own peculiar way. In the late 1880's and early 1890's a series of bulk freighters called whalebacks appeared. They looked almost exactly like floating cigars except their bows resembled pig snouts. Hence the nickname, pig boats.

Following the pig boat fad, lake freighters became a much more handsome breed. These were the prototypes of the freighters used today. The pilot house sits at the extreme fore and the propelling machinery at the extreme aft. The wide flat deck in between is the cargo space, with a multitude of hatches that can be thrown back to leave the hold almost completely open for easy loading and unloading. The efficient self-unloaders need no help from shore to clear out their cargo in a very short time. For approximately seven and one-half months each year the freighters transport iron ore, grain, limestone, coal and petroleum to and from Great Lakes' ports. A special kind of freighter is custom built to handle economically each major commodity.

In recent years new ships can be seen in the Soo

In April or May the ice breaks open and freighters are unleashed from their winter quarters. Viewed from above, they clear paths through huge lily pads of ice.

locks, rounding the Straits of Mackinac or docked in the larger harbors. These are the ocean vessels from nations around the earth. With the original St. Lawrence canals, only smaller crafts could enter the lakes. But when the St. Lawrence Seaway opened in 1959, the large lake cities became ports for the whole world's merchant fleet. This worldwide trade is an ever increasing source of wealth for the lakes.

The Great Lakes' fishing industry has fallen on hard times. For many years a wealth of whitefish, lake trout and walleyed pike supplied a delicious, thriving business. But at some unknown time — perhaps during the Ice Ages or, perhaps, when the

canals brought the ocean to the lakes — a super parasite invaded Lake Ontario. The eel-like sea lamprey has a head end like a circular suction cup. It locks onto the nearest big fish and gnaws a hole in the fish's side. The lamprey dines on the fish until it dies, then moves on to a new victim.

In the early 1930's Lake Erie fishermen began to find these loathsome creatures in their nets. Within a mere fifteen years, virtually all the whitefish and trout were gone from lakes Michigan, Huron, Erie and Ontario. And by the early 1950's the lampreys were successfully navigating the Soo locks or the

The shallowest of the Great Lakes, Lake Erie's often stormswept waters make navigation difficult for even large ships like the Sir William H. Truesdale. *This rare photo of the carrier, taken in the 1930's, captures the violence of waves crashing over the deck.*

St. Mary's River rapids. Soon half of Lake Superior's trout was destroyed.

Finally a frantic U.S. Fish and Wildlife Service found a cure. They knew that the lamprey spawned only in tributary streams to the Great Lakes. They developed a chemical that would kill the young lamprey in these streams before they reached the lakes. But the lampricide would not harm other fish. It was immediately rushed into Lake Superior streams in hopes of saving the few remaining trout. In 1962, one year after the lampricide was placed in all the streams, the lamprey population dropped by eighty-five percent. The lampricide program was continued to the other lakes. Soon trout and whitefish began to make a comeback.

Because the big fish had almost died out, the lakes produced an overabundance of little alewives. As the lakes have become stocked with new fish, the alewives have provided plenty of forage. The tough coho salmon, imported from Oregon, are growing at an astounding rate. This new game fish is luring a profusion of sport fishermen to the lake country. Even the commercial fisherman may someday soon net unlimited bounty once again.

If people do not pollute the lakes to death, their future looks bright. The copper industry has faded but iron ore is going strong. Man has replaced the forests. The new worldwide trade promises unlimited wealth. The fishing industry is rebounding.

But the most pleasant treasure of all is the lake country's own special beauties. Large tracts of public land have become recreational meccas for Canadian and American travelers. The sandy lakefronts draw beach buffs; campgrounds lure vacationers to the forests. Modern-day *voyageurs* portage through the isolated wilderness canoe routes. Hunters and fishermen pursue their game. Snowmobile trails and ski slopes attract winter sportsmen. The primitive splendor of Isle Royale National Park calls woodland hikers; the busy resorts on Traverse Bay appeal to less rustic visitors. A place to walk alone in the forest, a chance to sail a quiet bay. These are the greatest of the Great Lakes' gifts to man.

Land of the Changing Seasons

The Great Lakes country dramatically displays the changing of the seasons. This is not the climate for those who seek a year-round summer or perpetual cool. Each season stands fresh and pure and distinct with its own special joys.

Autumn is the amber season for the lakes. The upper Midwest, the northeastern United States and the provinces of Ontario and Quebec in Canada

have just the right climate for the brightest of color displays — sunny warm days and nights that chill to forty-five degrees and below.

Why do leaves change color? Some say it is the frost that does it. Others, more scientifically minded, know that the shorter days prohibit the green chlorophyll from soaking as much energy from the sun; then the yellow and orange carotenoids of the trees become the dominant hues. But perhaps an old Indian legend affords the most pleasing explanation: Long ago, godly hunters slew the Great Bear in the autumn of the year. In his death throes, his blood stained the forest, mottling the trees with red. As the hunters roasted his flesh, fat splattered into the woods, coating the rest of the leaves with yellow and gold. Each year, fall commemorates the demise of the Great Bear.

Because so much of the Great Lakes region is still tree-covered, fall colors here are unparalleled, from Minnesota's north woods to upper New York and the Gaspé Peninsula. Patches of evergreen mingle their deep, emerald hues with the saffron, bronze and red of the hardwoods. While color tours draw many to the Northern forests, the summer crowds are gone. Now is the time to be alone with the land and the music of thousands of migrating birds.

The deep woods are strafed with a spectrum of bright flashes as flickers, robins and blue jays retreat to the South. Flying high above are the large waterfowl, the Canada geese, sandhill cranes and endless varieties of ducks. Shy warblers travel in small flocks by night while nuthatches, downy woodpeckers and gray jays stay behind to greet the oncoming snow.

In autumn, nature does a bit of maintenance work on its grounds. As the fallen leaves decompose, they return to the earth the valuable elements which the trees originally borrowed from the soil. They also provide a rich, water-absorbing humus that promotes new growth. Beach grasses, now bronzed and lowered by frost, help stabilize the windblown sands.

In most lands, winter is a somber affair but in lake country it is a time of unearthly beauty. Early

Throughout Great Lakes country,
stolid oaks mingle their dusty red autumn
tones with the dancing gold
of aspen and birch.

Tom Algire

When the whole world seems locked in a deep freeze, the earth still retains some warmth. Seeping groundwater drips into crystalline ice stalactites in a Lake Superior cave on Wisconsin's Bayfield Peninsula.

Half-buried pines peak out from sleek snowdrifts. The winter is so cold in Michigan's Keweenaw Peninsula that snow becomes powdery with the billowing softness of sand dunes.

Joe Kirkish

in the season, piercing winds whip the lakes into a frenzy; they angrily pound their coasts, sculpting strange ice pillars and caves. Near the shore, every rock and plant will become sheathed in clear ice.

As time moves deeper into winter, the lakes freeze farther out from shore. Bays are ice jammed; harbors are closed. At Marquette, Michigan, temperatures have dropped as low as twenty-seven degrees below zero while the snowfall can build to twenty feet and more during a winter.

An eerie stillness spreads over the land. Ice stalactites form where creeks once ran; deep snows muffle every forest sound. Far to the north the Aurora Borealis puts on a spectacular color show for the timber wolves and chickadees and few other creatures that venture into the frozen world. The Great Lakes are locked in a deep freeze.

For northland creatures a hectic search for food begins. Before the snows get too deep, moose can dig down to the moss beneath. Afterwards, they must put their heads up to browse the branches of alder, aspen and maple. The deer, too, must subsist on what twigs they can reach in cedar, mountain ash and red osier. Black bears hibernate beneath

Canada dogwood (above) decorates the Isle Royale forest every spring. A russula mushroom (right) pushes through the mossy forest floor in Michigan's Upper Peninsula. Later, its top will curve upward like an umbrella caught in a strong wind.

the roots of blown-over trees, awakening only in warmer, sunny spells. Chipmunks feed from the stores of seeds and nuts they have gathered on gentler days, and foxes stalk the mice that bulldoze tunnels beneath the snow.

Then gradually the ice breaks and is gone. The St. Lawrence Seaway reopens and each mighty city and tiny town celebrates the arrival of the ships of spring. The season enters the scene in wild and fitful squalls; melt waters of ice jams and snow cushions rush through the streams and rivers, flooding their adjacent terrain. As the season settles down, its days grow sunnier and the first chartreuse leaves appear. Sun filters through them, dappling the forest floor. Suddenly a riotous carpet

of wildflowers covers the ground. Wild mushrooms peek out from their hiding places beneath decaying logs and leaves.

Dozens of game and songbirds return from their winter retreats. All animals tackle their spring chores. The beaver repairs his lodge, the chipmunk immediately starts storing food for the following winter and shorebirds comb the beaches for whatever is good in the winter-tossed debris. Life has begun again.

Spring oozes into the hot days of summer. Inland it is often muggy, but lake breezes cool the shores. Now the beaches go to work, hosting the winter-weary crowds. The lower lakes warm until swimmers can enjoy them where not seriously

polluted; Lake Superior does not. Away from shore, its open waters rarely warm above fifty degrees. That could drown even a strong swimmer in about fifteen minutes.

Along with the sunbathers come the ship captains. Every basin is jammed with gleaming yachts, every bay speckled with fishermen's dinghies and motorboats. Colorful sails dip and plunge as the famous summer sailing races, like July's annual Chicago to Mackinac race, call sailors to the lakes.

Lake country is never really still; if there are clouds in the sky, they will probably be moving. However, these breezes that modify the heat are not always a blessing because the Great Lakes are a stormy crew. Lake Superior, with its cold, deep waters, is by nature secretive and squally; those who know the lake never really trust it. It is the other Great Lakes that lull their visitors into a false sense of security. Their friendly warm waters lure the little boats far from shore. Then, in a matter of minutes, the wind can whip these lakes into catastrophic gales. The lower lakes are so shallow their waters are easily stirred. Many times Lake Erie has pitched so violently its lake bottom has been exposed in the gullies between the swells.

In some ways, Great Lakes' storms are more dangerous than those of the oceans. Not only do they give far less warning of their approach, but waves, rapidly rising to thirty and forty feet high, follow each other in quick succession. These

Charles M. Sheridan

Marsh marigolds, also known as cowslips, brighten a small shady brook. Their saffron blossoms are common in the spring in all the Great Lakes' swampier environs.

Unlike their domestic relatives, wild roses have almost no scent; only their color attracts the insects that distribute their pollen. Their bright pink dapples the early summer woods across the northern Great Lakes.

Joe Kirkish

choppy waves and narrow troughs batter the lake boats in a manner more frantic than do the ocean's long, rolling swells. A ship has no time to regain its balance from one water wall before another is upon it.

The Great Lakes, especially in the days before radio, racked up an incredible record of wrecked ships and lost crews. The history of the lakes is filled with tales of phantom ships whose remains have never been found. In one 1913 storm alone, a total of thirty-nine ships sank or were stranded; at least 250 sailors perished in the sixteen-hour-long gale. This storm was a November storm, but no month is without its death toll. November's cold winds coat a ship with hundreds of tons of ice, so a storm can easily sink it. No less lethal are the twisting fronts that boil up from the South and set the lakes to churning on a hot summer's night. Even at their deadliest, these storms are a beautiful and fearsome sight of nature gone berserk.

But the beauty is still there after the storm. You cannot really explain the loveliness of the Great Lakes' seasons. Only that sixth sense, the camera, can begin to record them. To know them, you must hear the haunting laughter of a summer loon. You must see the ice arches rise before a crystalline blue winter sky. To know the Great Lakes' seasons, you must go to them.

SUPERIOR
The Great Wilderness Lake

The French called it *Supérieur*, meaning the upper lake. To the British that would never do, so they twisted the meaning to denote significance and grandeur.

Both were right. Lake Superior is the northernmost of the Great Lakes, and its stark promontories, wild shores and violent waters also afford it the title of the grandest. It is the biggest freshwater lake in the world, covering nearly thirty-two thousand square miles. Superior is also the deepest of the Great Lakes, reaching a maximum depth of 1,333 feet.

Superior is unlike the lakes around it in its geology, too. Centuries ago explorers were noting its strange makeup. In 1823, Dr. John J. Bigsby wrote:

> Lake Superior differs widely from Lake Huron, in having a more regular outline, in having but few islands, in the grander features of its coasts, and in its geological structure, which, as far as I know, have no parallel in America.

The lake itself is young, emerging from the ice a very few thousand years ago. But its tough basin is made of some of the oldest and hardest rock in the world. Its northern shores expose lichen-quilted outcroppings of the Canadian Shield. This volcanic granite, quartz, slate and greenstone was laid down 2.5 billion years ago. In more recent years these old slabs were coated with the sands and gravels of the glacial melt waters. The volcanic age is largely responsible for the mineral wealth that lured men long ago. And it is responsible for luring men today; its ancient cliffs ring much of the lake, giving the islands and shores a rugged beauty that rivals any on earth.

The Indians also viewed Superior differently. To them, this lake was more than a source of food, a highway for canoes. Superior was the homeland of the gods. The Indians revered this entire waterway, its every rock formation and island.

During Superior's frequent storms, the Indians would throw it sacrifices — tobacco or their provisions — and implore the *Manitou*, or Spirit, of the waters to make the lake be still. According to Father Allouez, one of the earliest missionaries on these waters:

> During storms and tempests they sacrifice a dog, throwing it to the lake . . . At perilous places in the rivers, they propitiate the eddies and rapids by offering them presents.

Copper, as well as the waters, was revered by the Indians. It was a magical gift from the gods. They

Autumn's colors splotch the lake-scarred cliffs of Wisconsin's Bayfield Peninsula along Lake Superior's southwestern shore.

surrounded it with ritual and wore it in their medicine bags. Hence, Isle Royale became a sacred place because of the *caignetdaze*, or copper, the Chippewa found there. They tried to protect their magic island from the European advance by telling eerie tales about it. Some completely denied its existence, saying it was merely a myth. Others claimed it was a shadowy mass that vaporized here and there. Still others swore that to set foot on it was to die. But the whites eventually came and took the island anyway; they, too, worshiped the copper but for very different reasons.

Many beautiful Chippewa legends explain how the lake's features and shore came to be. One day, according to one tale, a great *Manitou* was pursuing a tremendous stag. Each arrow he shot missed his fleet prey. The deer finally reached the shore of Lake Superior and plunged in, leaving the *Manitou* behind. From the shore, the angry Spirit flung great fistfuls of rock at the escaping deer. The rocks sprinkled over the lake to become Wisconsin's Apostle Islands.

Another Chippewa Spirit created the magnificent Pictured Rocks, apparently for his own pleasure. This, of course, was a most laborious chore and, upon completion, the weary *Manitou* required a lengthy rest. He lay down to slumber in the cool waters of Munising Bay, next to the Pictured Rocks. He sleeps there still, his form the beautiful Grand Island.

The best known stories of the upper lake spring from Henry Wadsworth Longfellow's imaginative but inaccurate epic, *Song of Hiawatha.* The *Gitche Gumee*, or Big-Sea-Water, of the poem is Lake Superior, and Hiawatha's passage is marked along its southern shores. However, it wasn't Hiawatha, the name of an Iroquois chief, who had traveled this wilderness. The legendary hero that Longfellow described was a Chippewa demigod named Manabozho. Longfellow had heard the tale from Henry Rowe Schoolcraft, Michigan's first ethnologist, who had heard it from his Chippewa wife who had heard it during her childhood in the Apostle Islands. Somewhere along the line, like most rumors, the story went awry. Hence, the chief Hiawatha has been immortalized for deeds Manabozho did.

A logical way to tour Lake Superior is to begin at Sault Ste. Marie, Ontario, and follow the lake's 2,796-mile-long shore all the way around and back to Sault Ste. Marie, Michigan. The lake's Canadian border is rimmed by the Trans-Canada Highway. This drive alternately moves inland then skirts the shore, passing through the most beautiful country on earth. Between the few major settlements on the route — Wawa, Schreiber, Thunder Bay — much of the country is as wild as the days the first *voyageurs* paddled the northern bays.

Several Ontario provincial parks border Lake Superior, but the lakeland of Canada is still lovely even where it is not being protected; the scenery outside the parks rivals the scenery within. Twenty-foot waves pound the ancient coast; in wilder storms, forty-foot mounds have thundered to land. Vast tracks of deep evergreen forest shield the deer and moose that rummage through the north woods.

The first park just outside of Sault Ste. Marie is little Batchawana Bay Picnic Ground. This forty-acre recreation provincial park offers picnic grounds only; no campers are allowed here. Its sandy beach is a respite for sunbathers, but its waters are for only the hardiest of swimmers; Lake Superior is much too cold for most.

Pancake Bay, forty-eight miles north of Sault Ste. Marie, is a fine example of a recreation provincial park that allows camping. The park stretches between Highway 17 and the Superior shore. Two sandy miles of beach plus modern tent and trailer sites lure hundreds of campers to its 1,151 acres.

Of the four remaining parks that rim the lake, three are natural environment provincial parks and one is a national park. They reserve natural and historic landscapes, but they also provide more opportunities for outdoor recreation. Hiking, canoeing and studying nature are permitted throughout these parks. Modern facilities make the main campgrounds quite comfortable while remote areas provide more rugged facilities for those who like to "rough it." A careful watch is maintained to guard the balance between the park services and the natural attractions.

Lake Superior Provincial Park, eighty-five miles from Sault Ste. Marie, is the largest on the lake. Its 526 square miles house hundreds of lakes, Old Woman River, Sand River and its falls, plus innumerable trout streams. The rest of the park is comprised of picturesque hills, sprinkled with pine and hardwood forest, accessible by hiking and nature study trails.

One of the most striking features of the park is the Indian Rock Paintings on the sheer cliffs of Lake Superior's Agawa Bay. The thirty-five Agawa Rock pictographs say that an Indian war party came in five canoes from the south shore of Lake Superior to destroy an enemy village near Agawa.

Mysterious picture writings like these can be found in several places in Superior country. They

The zigzagging north shore of Lake Superior, product of hundreds of Pre-Cambrian lava flows, rivals the New England coast in grandeur. The large, rounded mound in the distance is Palisade Head.

are generally high in the cliffs surrounding the lake. Their hieroglyphics represent animals, canoes, men and unrecognizable designs. Exactly when they were done is unknown and their messages are still only half deciphered; most seem to be stories about gods and battles. Some are carved where the rock is soft. Others are painted with a long-lasting red pigment. Near Marathon, Ontario, the Indians used yet a third method. Dr. Bigsby described these Written Rocks, called *Les Ecrits*, in 1823:

> They are seven miles west of the Black River. They occur in a cluster of islets close to a large headland of glaring red colour, like all in this vicinity . . . the drawings are made by simply detaching the dark lichens from the flat surface of the rock. At their

west end there is a good representation of an Indian firing at two animals . . . .

Between Lake Superior Provincial Park and Marathon, the Trans-Canada Highway goes far inland, away from Superior. The land between them has become Pukaskwa National Park, one of the newest national parks in Canada. Pukaskwa encompasses 725 square miles of north woods, highlands, waterfalls, lakes, bays and rivers. For the first time in a Canadian park, the Chippewa Indians are taking an active hand in Pukaskwa's development.

(continued on page 58)

Overleaf: *Bathing ancient rocks and pebbles to bring out their rusty brown and gray tones, the icy waters of Lake Superior break on the Minnesota coast.*

Two thousand years ago, semi-nomadic peoples fished for a living on a sandy plain overlooking Lake Superior. They were the first to enjoy what is now Neys Provincial Park. Neys, sixteen miles west of Marathon, has a rather ignoble modern history as a prisoner of war camp in World War II. German prisoners and Japanese internees were brought here to these isolated woods. They were set to work as lumberjacks, and paid the going rate of fifty cents a cord per day plus two dollars for every cord over six in a week. Apparently the prisoners made the best of it in their northern lock-up; they built ice skating rinks and the various camps challenged

shows long parallel scratches made by materials shoved over them by glaciers. The park has a mile-long sand beach, and fishermen stalk Northern pike in its western boundary, the Little Pic River. Self-guided nature trails criss-cross the park; an early morning hike might be rewarded with sightings of moose and deer, fox and mink. Very rarely seen is the small herd of caribou that frequents the park.

Not far from Neys is the little recreation provincial park of Rainbow Falls. While it is not actually on Lake Superior, a lookout point within its grounds offers a fine view of the lake's shoreline

Les Blacklock   Michigan Tourist Council

each other to soccer matches. One camp always brought along its mascot — a bear trained in German. Many of the Germans, sent home after the war, returned to the Canadian woods as permanent settlers.

The area around these old camps was reserved as Neys Provincial Park in 1962. Today, a few foundations of prison camp buildings and remnants of barbed wire fencing can still be seen in the sand dunes behind the trailer campgrounds.

The rocky, round-topped hills that surround the campgrounds are coated with lush pine forests. In the few areas where the hills are exposed, the rock

and islands. Its camping facilities are a bit more modern than many of Neys' rustic sites.

Twenty-four miles east of Thunder Bay is Sibley, Lake Superior's second biggest provincial park. The wilderness here is ninety-four square miles of the northland's prettiest country. Sibley is a small peninsula dipping into the cold waters of far north Lake Superior. Its rugged lakefront rock formations are backed by thick pine forests; no other park arouses a more acute feeling of being surrounded by wild things.

The hulking shape of a huge rock formation called Sleeping Giant projects from the tip of the

Sibley peninsula. Off the coast of the park is little Silver Islet. In 1868, this speck of rock — only eighty feet at its widest — touched off its very own mineral boom. The incredibly tiny island produced $3,250,000 worth of silver, while very little was found elsewhere in the vicinity.

Minnesota has a 150-mile coastline between Duluth and the Pigeon River, which forms the Canada-United States border. This stretch of land is studded with volcanic cliffs; the rocky shore is as lovely as any New England has to offer. The lake is the southeast border of Minnesota's Arrowhead country. Between the lake and the Canadian

Little of the original red and white pine is left, but the second-growth timber is a lush mixture of fir, spruce and jack pine. Aspen and birch stand tall over the mossy remains of the felled monarchs; pale green lichens clutch the weathered boulders of the ancient volcanic granite jutting up from the woodland floor. The forest is dark and rich, the lakes pure and the air clean.

At the north end of the forest, adjacent to Ontario's vast Quetico Provincial Park, is the Boundary Waters Canoe Area, the largest water-based wild area in the country. It is the primitive heart of one of the last true wilderness remnants in

The most widely distributed deer in the United States, the white-tailed deer is abundant everywhere around Lake Superior. This handsome buck (opposite) sports a thick winter coat while a younger deer (above) wades a shoreline stream.

border sprawls Superior National Forest, covering over three million acres and most of the Arrowhead, the largest national forest in the contiguous United States.

Superior National Forest is a working preserve. Timber is harvested on a sustained yield basis; gravel pits and iron-ore mines dot the commercial areas. But as you move away from the settled sections, the forest rolls for miles, interrupted only by a sprinkling of inland lakes.

the United States. Here, America's last viable population of Eastern timber wolf avoids human intervention. Here, too, the bald and golden eagles seek their lonely retreats. Superior National Forest is, indeed, a spectacular backdrop for the state parks on Minnesota's north shore.

At the far northern tip of the Arrowhead is a commemoration to the great fur trade of the 1700's. Grand Portage National Monument was established in 1960 to protect the portage that skirts a twenty-mile series of rapids near the mouth of the Pigeon River.

Grand Portage existed centuries before the fur traders. Prehistoric Indians first wore the narrow path as the easiest route around the rapids. The traders naturally followed the same trail. Thousands of tons of furs and trade goods crossed the nine-mile portage on *voyageurs'* backs.

The North West Company established a post at the east end of the trail, on the Lake Superior shore, and named it, too, Grand Portage. This was the first white settlement in Minnesota. At this post the traders, interpreters, *voyageurs* and guides met each July to exchange their furs, trade goods and tall tales. Here, too, they received — and for the most part spent — their annual wages.

Today the trail is much the same as it was two centuries ago, only now it bisects the reservation of the Grand Portage Band of the Minnesota Chippewa Tribe. Hidden springs and mossy rocks line the forested trail. A stockade, Great Hall and gate house have been reconstructed to give Grand Portage a flavor of the bygone settlement that once reigned the upper lake.

The numerous state parks lining the north shore are mirrors of how the land must have looked once. Their purpose is to preserve the original identity of the region. In geologic time, first came the hundreds of lava flows that crossed over each other. This irregular terrain became still more uneven as glacial ice broke it up. The many rivers and streams running into Lake Superior have to cross these jagged dropoffs and rugged gorges. That is why almost every state park here has a waterfall or rapids plunging to the lake. Some are high tumbling falls; others are series of stairsteps; all are beautiful.

Judge C. R. Magney State Park, eighteen miles northeast of Grand Marais, offers a most intriguing waterfall. It can be reached via a picturesque hike up the boiling waters of the Brule River. As Pothole Falls, also known as Devils Kettle Falls, cascades downward, its waters are divided by a rocky protrusion. Part of the water tumbles seventy feet, then continues on its way. The rest is a mystery. Just as it begins to pour over the lip of the falls, it disappears into a pothole about ten feet in diameter. Exactly where and how this water rejoins the other half of the river is still unknown.

About forty miles southeast of Judge C. R. Magney is another park featuring a tremendous pothole in the rocky river gorge of Temperance River. It is a round, smooth hole that has been drilled into the rock by sand grains suspended in the fast, swirling water. Both Judge C. R. Magney

and Temperance River state parks supplement the scenery of their rock-walled rivers with modern campsites, foot trails and superb stream fishing.

The highest waterfall in Minnesota is found in Baptism River State Park, thirty-three miles northeast of Two Harbors. Several smaller falls add to the park's appeal. Fast water winds through twisting rocky gorges in Cascade River State Park and Cross River State Wayside. Caribou Falls, Kodunce River and Devils Track State Wayside all feature rugged gorges and falls. (State waysides are typically smaller than the state parks and are generally geared for daytime picnickers.)

One of the prettiest parks on the coast is Gooseberry Falls State Park. The river here was once named for an early French fur trader. However, the British couldn't pronounce "Groseilliers" so they changed it to Gooseberry. The park of 740 acres is just thirteen miles northeast of Two Harbors. Its Lake Superior cliffs are as scenic as any on the north shore, and the Gooseberry River here is riddled with white water. Two separate falls are the namesake for the park where the evidence of glaciers is especially visible; the grooves in the rock surfaces give testimony to the scraping of passing ice. A naturalist resides in the park in the summer to conduct nature study tours and evening interpretive programs. In the winter, snowmobilers are allowed on designated trails.

The most spectacular event in the park takes place in the fall when Gooseberry Falls, as well as Baptism River, Temperance River and Cascade River state parks — all within about sixty miles of each other — are front row seats for the annual hawk migration. The hills to one side and the lake to the other cause the magnificent birds to funnel through this area, exactly over the parks. Nowhere in the states is another migration as impressive as this one.

All the parks of the Minnesota north shore are excellent for birdwatchers. In the summer, the boreal forests are alive with the sweet music of many species of warblers, thrushes and vireos. Flood Bay State Wayside, a tiny park eleven miles southwest of Gooseberry Falls, is a fine stance for winter observation of the rare glaucous and Iceland gulls. This little park offers one of the very few sandy beaches on the rockbound coast of the Minnesota shore.

(continued on page 63)

The highest light in America, Split Rock Lighthouse is now a state park. It was built in 1909 of materials delivered by water and lifted up the 178-foot cliff.

These parks are also excellent preserves for a wide variety of wildflowers; Lake Superior modifies their climate a bit more than the inland parks. So here you'll find a profusion of flowering raspberry and lungwort, rare lady slippers and wild sarsaparilla. Lungwort, a cluster of blue bells, was once thought valuable as a cure for respiratory troubles; hence, its name.

This area was settled by Scandinavians years ago. From their homeland they brought flashy yellow European buttercups and ox-eye daisies. Even the smallest of wayside parks, like Ray Bergland and undeveloped Devils Track, are carpeted with bright wildflowers every spring.

Two parks remain to be seen for their unique attractions. George H. Crosby Manitou State Park, about fifteen miles northeast of Silver Bay, is a 4,790-acre primitive park. This is the largest of the Minnesota north shore parks and one of the wildest. Backpacking trails bisect the lush forests; two waterfalls urge the Manitou River to the lake, and this is a favorite park of those who like to snowshoe. Then hikers can find tracks of the rare fisher in the early morning, new-fallen snows.

Fourteen miles northeast of Gooseberry Falls is Split Rock Lighthouse State Park. The purpose of the grounds is to preserve the historic old lighthouse as a symbol of the north shore. For sixty years, beginning in 1909, the light in its octagonal building guided mariners into the Duluth harbor. Perched on the steep cliffs 178 feet above the lake, it is still the highest light in the United States and its beam could be seen for twenty-two miles when it was in operation. The view from this park is one of the finest anywhere on the Lake Superior shore.

Wisconsin has a rather brief shoreline on the lake, but Apostle Islands National Lakeshore, one of the most remarkable areas anywhere on the

Icicles drip from the Apostle Islands where winds and waves have sculpted the coast into unique overhanging cliffs. Lichens and chemicals in seeping groundwater have stained the rock red.

Wisconsin Department of Natural Resources

The pine, aspen, maple and birch forest of the Apostle Islands (above) creeps to the shore. A pillar in the Apostles (opposite) is the result of centuries of erosion.

lakes, was established in Wisconsin in 1970. It includes twenty of the twenty-two islands in an archipelago off the Bayfield Peninsula. The islands range in size from three-acre Gull Island to ten-thousand-acre Stockton Island. Also within the bounds of the national lakeshore are eleven miles of coast on the mainland.

The park is so new that land purchasing is still in the early stages. The same is true of planning. At this time, it appears that the islands will be left as wild and picturesque as they now are. Only

limited, very primitive campsites will be developed on a few of the islands for loners and explorers. Presently, several new sites are available on Stockton Island. The mainland acreage will be developed to provide more convenient camping, hiking and boating facilities.

There are two theories on how the Apostles were named. Some say a band of pirates lived in a secluded cave on an outer island. They called

(continued on page 67)

Les Blacklock

themselves the Apostles and claimed their booty from the earliest Lake Superior ships. The other theory, if less colorful, is more logical. A Jesuit missionary climbed to a high point on the mainland and overlooked the islands before him. He could see only twelve and reverently named them the Apostles.

He did not, however, bother to name any islands for particular Apostles. The names most of them have been given are simply translations of the original Indian names — islands like Otter, Raspberry, Devil, Oak and Gull. Only Manitou Island was allowed to keep its Indian appelation, maybe out of respect for the Indian spirits. Henry Rowe Schoolcraft, Michigan's earliest Indian agent, believed they should be named for the states but he only succeeded in making two names, York and Michigan, stick. Hermit Island was dubbed for an unpopular man who was run out of town by the late nineteenth-century settlers of Madeline Island (so called for the daughter of a Chippewa chief, White Crane). He lived on the island all alone, supposedly burying a great hoard of silver and gold coins. For years, adventurers searched in vain for the hidden treasure.

Indians lived quietly for many centuries on these islands; some of the most ancient Lake Superior evidences have been found here. About the time Columbus arrived in the New World, the Chippewas were building a fort on Long Island, a narrow strip that helps protect Chequamegon Bay from Lake Superior's fitful storms. Shortly after the French began to arrive at the islands, the Indians left them. Somehow, the rumor spread among the Indians that the spirits of the dead warriors they had slain in battle and then eaten, as was their habit, haunted the islands. They decided it would be wise to abandon them for awhile.

The missionaries followed the earliest explorers. Seven great Indian nations had headquarters here and first heard the Christian message. Their runners carried it from village to village until the Word

*Gusty winds force whitecaps to smack
the shores of Michigan's Keweenaw Peninsula.
This is the great copper country, as
rich in ore as it is in scenery.*

Ken Dequaine

Tom Algire

Whitecaps spray the rocky shoreline (opposite)
of Au Train Bay west of Munising. Jutting into Lake
Superior's belly, Eagle Harbor lighthouse (above),
built in 1871, identifies the Keweenaw Peninsula
for ships that pass in the fog or the night.

reached as far west as the Rocky Mountains, and as far east as western Virginia.

White men have done their best to destroy the Apostles but the islands have fought back and won. Commercial groups didn't last long. The American Fur Company was posted here but withdrew when the company folded. Lumberjacks skimmed off the best timber but the second growth is now as lush as the first. Quarrymen bit into the sandstone but their quarries are now overgrown. A few broken remains can be seen on Stockton Island. Only a handful of commercial fishermen remain to dip their living from the icy waters around the islands.

So the Apostles today stand wild and free, under Government protection. Only the waters and wind assault them now, digging new sea arches and thunder caves and rocky colonnades along their rugged shore. Lush green forests of pine, hazelnut and mountain ash top the red-rock boulders. These jagged ledges and caverns are a spectacular joy for sightseers and photographers. They can best be seen on the boat tours that leave from Bayfield. The Chippewa tribe at the nearby Red Cliff Indian Reservation operates charter boats for fishing among the islands.

The largest Apostle, Madeline Island, is not included in the national lakeshore. This island is inhabited to a considerable extent and its main village, La Pointe, is easily reached by car ferry from Bayfield. La Pointe is primarily a tourist town, featuring charter boats, a museum of local history and an Indian burial ground. Originally, small wooden structures were built over the graves to protect the deceased in the world beyond. These graves have made it through two centuries but recent vandalism has destroyed several of the fragile structures.

Madeline Island is the site of Wisconsin's only Lake Superior state park. Big Bay State Park is also one of the newest and is still being developed. It is about midway along the island's southeast coast and features a one-and-a-half-mile-long sand beach butted up against one and a half miles of rock formation, caves and ledges. Its beach is a barrier that protects an island lagoon, and this fine marshland is a wildlife refuge and an excellent fishing ground.

Michigan has the longest border of any state on Lake Superior. In fact, if you total up the length of Michigan's Great Lakes shores, it amounts to more miles than there are along America's entire Atlantic seaboard. Wherever you are in Michigan, you are never more than six miles from some body of water. And since the state is still half covered with trees, it offers thousands of fine campsites.

Michigan's westernmost state park along the Lake Superior shore is the largest. Porcupine Mountains Wilderness State Park is fifty-eight thousand acres of wild rivers, isolated lakes and virgin timber. The park is rife with tumbling falls like those on the rapid Presque Isle River.

While Superior's south shore is generally flatter than its north, the "Porkies" are the highest mountains in the Midwest. Winding scenic drives reach a few of the park's most appealing sites, but to really see the Porcupines, you must be a hiker. Many of the park's charms are secluded at the ends of rugged wilderness trails.

Hidden in the heights of the mountains is little Mirror Lake, the highest lake in Michigan at 1,531 feet. Three other lakes are secluded in the wilds; two of them can be reached only from backpacking trails. The third, and possibly the loveliest, can be seen a short walk from the road. Far below the escarpment where you will stand is Lake of the Clouds.

The longest trail in the park is the sixteen-mile Lake Superior Trail which follows the lakeshore. For those who wish to ford the many streams and traverse the rough coast, this trail presents the park's most spectacular scenery.

Porcupine Mountains Wilderness State Park is one of Michigan's busiest winter parks. Rope tows,

Ed Simpson

T-bars and a chair lift tote skiers to the open slopes and trails. Snowshoeing and snowmobiling are both increasingly popular pastimes.

Three lakefront state parks grace Michigan's Keweenaw Peninsula, a finger of land jutting about eighty miles into Lake Superior. It was the heartland of the Michigan copper boom in the mid-nineteenth century. The old Arcadian Copper Mine near Hancock is now open to the public for a close view of early ore operations.

Centuries before white miners scrambled over the peninsula seeking out ore, Indians mined the Keweenaw copper. No burial grounds or village remains have been found, indicating that they came here only seasonally to take copper for their own use and for trade. Copper which has certain characteristics peculiar to Keweenaw copper has been found as far south as Alabama.

Eleven billion pounds of copper have been mined from this narrow strip of land; several mines are still operating, but most are gone. Hidden in the forests are rusting shaft houses, tram cars and quiet ghost towns. Stacks of rejected "poor rock" surround the decaying remains.

The Keweenaw is Upper Michigan's prettiest country. The forests are a mixture of pine and hardwood; in the fall the bright yellow and orange of birch and maple dance before the sedate green background of spruce and fir. The summertime trees canopy the roads that travel the length of the peninsula. The shoreline is a rugged zig-zag of volcanic rock brutalized by wind and waves, breaking it into hanging ledges and jagged shards.

At the tip of the Keweenaw is Fort Wilkins State Park. The fort was originally built to protect the miners from the Chippewa, but the Indians never were a problem. Primarily the troops protected the miners from other miners, claim jumpers and illegal liquor salesmen; the fort was the only symbol of law and order for miles around. The officers had to control their soldiers as well as the miners. As the fort commander, Captain R. E. Clary, wrote in

1844: "The health of the command still remains excellent, and as we are no longer cursed by whiskey sellers, we have reasonable grounds to expect its continuance."

Today the fort has been restored as a 190-acre state park between Lake Fanny Hooe and Lake Superior. The barracks, officers' quarters and other fort buildings are open to the public. A shaft of an old copper mine is on the park grounds, as well as an historical museum, modern campsites and naturalist-guided hikes and evening programs.

F. J. McLain and Baraga state parks are also Keweenaw campgrounds. McLain is a favorite base camp for rockhounds, especially agate fanciers. They remove hundreds of pounds of stone each year from the peninsula's gravel beaches and old mine dumps. The park, ten miles northwest of Hancock, fronts Lake Superior and Bear Lake, with long, sandy beaches on both. Its central location makes it a good starting point to visit the rest of the Keweenaw.

Baraga State Park was named for the missionary, Frederic Baraga. Beginning in 1835, the Catholic priest roamed Lake Superior's south shore for thirty years. He started his work with the Indians of the Apostle Islands and Chequamegon Bay area. Then he moved to Sault Ste. Marie where he

The wolf (opposite) is the object of ill-founded myths and fears and has been ruthlessly destroyed wherever possible. At Isle Royale National Park it is protected from such extermination. In fact, the wolves at Isle Royale, roaming in packs (below), have proved beneficial by helping to keep the moose population in ecological balance.

Ken Dequaine

became a bishop. From there, he was transferred to Houghton, the heart of the Keweenaw copper country.

The campground in Baraga State Park is a modern one that receives heavy use. It has a rocky, pebbly shore for beachcombers to enjoy. The park is located near the town of L'Anse, in the tip of the inland recess of Keweenaw Bay.

Twenty-two miles from Lake Superior's north shore (but now part of Michigan) is an elongated island of over half a million acres which the Indians tried to hide, but the French found anyway. Brulé may well have seen it in 1618; by 1664, Pierre Boucher noted its existence in his *History of Canada*. Loyal to Louis XIV, the French dubbed it Isle Royale.

Although discovered early, the island remained Chippewa land for another 150 years. As it passed from French to British to American hands, only a few fishermen and trappers ventured to its shores.

The great copper rush to the Keweenaw in the 1840's stimulated active interest in Isle Royale. Prospectors crossed the fifty-mile span from the south shore to the island to stake their claims. They burned the forests to expose outcroppings of ore, then blasted away at the ancient rock. They located the four-thousand-year-old diggings of ancient Indian mines and chipped away for anything the Indians may have missed. Shanty towns soon sprang up along the coast. Tracks were laid for a horse-drawn cart railway to service the island's most famous mine, the Minong. This rich lode operated about ten years; a single nugget weighed six hundred pounds. When it closed in the mid-1880's, it was all over. Today the shafts stand in empty, lonely decay.

The island became Isle Royale National Park in 1940. The years have corrected the miners' errors, and a new hardwood and pine forest has grown. Frequent rains give the forest the deep lushness for which Isle Royale is famous. The mossy carpet of the woodland floor is spotted with hundreds of wildflower species.

Wildlife abounds, too. Anything that can fly, swim or cross the fifteen miles of ice from Canada has found a protected home here. Beaver, once decimated by trappers, are plentiful. Some time around 1900 a moose herd crossed to the island. Wolves cull the herd and keep it to a population

Miners Castle (opposite) is one of the most spectacular formations at Pictured Rocks National Lakeshore. Nearby, Chapel Rock (above right) is continually carved by the curling pattern of erosive waves.

National Park Service

the island can support. Hikers can often see moose browsing through reedy lake bottoms. However, it is very rare to sight a wolf; they tend to steer clear of their only enemy, man.

More than 160 miles of foot trails criss-cross the island. There are no roads here; the only way to get from one end to the other is to boat around the island or hike over it. Many of the modern facilities offered in other parks do not exist on Isle Royale. It will be left as wild as possible.

A forty-five-mile hike covers the length of the island, following the backbone, Greenstone Ridge. To either side of the island's ridge, valleys slope downward to the coast and it provides stunning

Tumbling down layers of sandstone, quartz and shale, Bridal Veil Falls (above) cascades to Lake Superior in Pictured Rocks National Lakeshore. Forced upward when wind and water currents rearranged frozen formations, an ice pillar (opposite) towers above the bleak winter landscape.

views of inland lakes and rich forests. Beyond the Superior shore you can see a necklace of tiny islets that ring the main island and Canada to the north. A few primitive shelters have been constructed along the way; hikers often backpack one way, then return by boat.

At the northeast end of the island is Rock Harbor; to the southwest is Windigo. Boat taxis shuttle between the two villages. At the entrance of Rock Harbor is a reminder of the copper era, an old lighthouse built in 1855. The island can be reached by boat from Houghton and Copper Harbor on the Keweenaw, and from Grand Portage in Minnesota.

On the mainland, east of the Keweenaw Peninsula, is the western segment of Hiawatha National Forest. Most of the two-part woodland's 837,000

acres were forested and burned over in the lumbering era; today a rich second growth is again producing timber as well as a protected home for wild creatures. The forest borders lakes Michigan and Huron as well as Superior; more will be said about it in later chapters.

The Pictured Rocks, just northeast of Munising, is one of the south shore's unique attractions. Pictured Rocks National Lakeshore, established in 1958, is a Federal preserve still being developed. The lakeshore includes the fifteen-mile-long Pictured Rocks, twelve miles of sandy beach and five miles of the Grand Sable Banks and Dunes. The Pictured Rocks, a multicolored sandstone escarpment, rises as high as two hundred feet above Lake Superior. Layers of crystalline quartz, pebbles, blue slate, hard white dolomite and yellow limo-

(continued on page 77)

Joe Kirkish

A hazy sun descends over Lake Superior's Michigan shoreline. As winter approaches, ice coats the shoreline rocks and the water temperature tumbles to the point where it could freeze a man in less than sixty seconds.

nite cross the pink and brown sandstone cliffs. On a sunny day, all these colors glimmer brightly. In the spring, a profusion of waterfalls tumble over the rocks into blue Lake Superior far below. The rough waters, wind and frost constantly assault the escarpment, carving new thunder caves, arches and columns. The most famous formation of the Pictured Rocks, Miner's Castle, can be reached by car; the rest can best be seen from the boat tours out of Munising or by hiking the inland trails.

The Twelve-Mile Beach forms the middle segment of Pictured Rocks National Lakeshore. This area is still undeveloped; only primitive campsites are presently available. Lake Superior's waters are too cold for lengthy swims, but the sand and pebble shore is enjoyable for sunbathing and beachcombing. Thirty-foot sand bluffs rise above the beach for most of its length.

Grand Sable Banks, near the town of Grand Marais, Michigan, is a geological oddity. It was largely formed by lakebed sediments of a shallow sea that pre-dates Lake Superior. Glaciers sheared off the banks, coating them with debris. Now they rise 275 feet above the lake at a stark thirty-five-degree angle.

On the top of the banks are the Grand Sable Dunes. These sandy giants add eighty-five feet to the Grand Sable formations, and they cover an area of five square miles. They may well have begun as the sand shores of that ancient shallow sea. Now the wind off Lake Superior continually erodes surrounding sandstone formations, adding to their bulk. It tries to blow the dunes away from the shore, but inland vegetation partially stabilizes the movement.

Most of the 73,653 acres of Pictured Rocks National Lakeshore consists of a rich inland forest which acts as a buffer zone to protect the shore. The forest, once burned over, is largely inaccessible by road. So today, it is an uninterrupted wilderness of hardwood and pine. One large area is a pure stand of beautiful white birch. Falls, ponds, bogs and streams dot the forest. The abundance of water and ground cover hosts large populations of beaver, black bear, mink and white-tailed deer. Occasionally moose and lynx are sighted in the woods, where secluded lakes hold perch, smallmouth bass and Northern pike. The forest will largely be left alone to remain one of Michigan's finest wilderness stands.

Muskallonge Lake State Park, less than twenty miles east of Grand Marais, is in one of Michigan's wildest areas. The 172-acre park is a long narrow strip of land — not more than 1,500 feet — between Lake Superior and Muskallonge Lake, once a mill pond for thousands of white pine logs. The park is on the site of Deer Park, a bygone lumbering town of the 1800's. The boom town settlers depleted the forests by the 1900's, so they closed their mill, boarded up their stores and abandoned their shanty homes. Today all that is left to tell their tale is a huge pile of sawdust and submerged saw logs.

Michigan's second largest Lake Superior state park is noted more for its falls than its lakeshore. Tahquamenon Falls State Park offers campsites and beaches where its river reaches the Superior shore of Whitefish Bay. But the rough water upriver is what most people come to see.

Tahquamenon Falls is a two-part cascade. The Upper Falls drops forty feet and is two hundred feet wide at the crest. East of the Mississippi, only Niagara Falls is bigger than Tahquamenon. The Lower Falls are a beautiful tumbling stairway of gold-tinted water. An islet in the river provides an excellent view of this waterfall. Below the falls, the river flows more slowly through quiet swamps and between the park's high hills. This is beautiful canoe country. While most of the Tahquamenon forest was once harvested, some was not. Many of the trees in the fine climax forest are over three hundred years old.

Along the southern shore of Whitefish Bay, Hiawatha National Forest once again touches on Lake Superior. Here four campgrounds will be included in the forest's proposed Big-Sea-Water Recreation Area. Roxberry Creek, Bayview and Big Pine recreation sites are in various stages of completion; Monocle Lake Recreation Site, seven miles northwest of Brimley, is now supporting active use. A lakeshore drive is being constructed to run the length of the proposed recreation area.

The last park on the Lake Superior circuit, Brimley State Park, just twelve miles southwest of Sault Ste. Marie, offers a small sandy beach on Whitefish Bay. The 151-acre park is quite well developed and supports heavy usage.

For North Americans who love wilderness, it is becoming painfully rare. However unnatural it seems to live without it, we've let it slip away. But the wild places remain around the pure waters of Lake Superior. The upper lake is the grandest. See it while you still can.

Richard Parks

MICHIGAN
Great Water of the Heartland

The Ojibways named it *Mishi Sagie Gan*, the Great Water or Lake. It is the third largest Great Lake and the only one located totally within the United States.

The waters of Lake Michigan, 321 miles long, 118 miles wide, cover approximately 22,300 square miles and reach a depth of 923 feet. Great stretches of its coast border America's densely populated heartland, but to the north, sections of Lake Michigan are almost as wild as Superior. So the lake offers a diversity of sights and delights for everyone from luxury seekers to nature lovers.

The Straits of Mackinac, between the Upper and Lower peninsulas of Michigan, are the major egress for Lake Michigan. In the five-mile-wide alley of swift currents, the waters of Michigan mingle with Huron. Here, the blue-green lakes are forever coated with an icing of whitecaps. The straits, pockmarked with lovely and historic sights, have always been a major shipping channel. Just as they drew *voyageurs* hundreds of years ago, the giant lake ships quietly ply their waters today.

Northwest of the straits, the coastline of the Upper Peninsula meets Hiawatha National Forest; on both sides of Manistique, U.S. Route 2 wends through the protected woodlands. Limber aspen and birch rise through stolid spruce and fir to

A limber young tree piercing the yellow sky fights to gain a tenuous foothold in the slippery, moving sands of Indiana Dunes National Lakeshore.

dance in the lake winds. Their bright autumn hues color the inland side of the highway where it parallels the sandy beaches and low dunes of northern Lake Michigan. The forest service operates one small campground, Lake Michigan Recreation Site, to take advantage of this excellent beach.

Lake Michigan is studded with few sizable islands, but its biggest is the site of a unique chapter of Great Lakes history. Beaver Island is about twenty miles southeast of Seul Chois Point (this point was named "Only Choice" by the French because its cove was the only shelter for explorers and *voyageurs* between Epoufette and Manistique). In 1849, the island became a Mormon colony. The leader, James Jesse Strang, had received a revelation that the "land amidst wide waters" would be a fine home for his religious followers. The settlers farmed the island and fished the lake; they sold fuel to the woodburning steamers that passed their way. They named their settlement St. James in honor of their leader. When, in the summer of 1850, Strang crowned himself king of Beaver Island, the little land became the only island kingdom with its own monarch ever to exist in the United States.

The kingdom grew to two thousand while Strang ruled with a tight rein. But the Mormons' aggressive actions and foreign ways stirred trouble on the mainland. They had driven any "gentile" settler off the island; they were accused of pirating passing ships. Neighboring non-Mormons were scandalized by Strang's four wives. Eventually, his harsh practices lost favor even among his own people.

As lovely in winter as on warmer days, Cave Point's rocky coast is glossed with ice and snow cakes. This Door Peninsula limestone is a rib of the Niagara Escarpment.

They shot him on the St. James waterfront in 1856. Then mainland settlers swarmed over the island to burn Strang's tabernacle and drive the Mormons away.

Today, Beaver Island is inhabited by a handful of farmers and fishermen. In the summers, a boat from Charlevoix pays the island a daily visit. Hunters and backpackers roam the island because, by and large, it has returned to the wilderness. Only the tattered remains of old Mormon homes recall its days as an island kingdom.

Michigan has preserved another historical era in Fayette State Park. Fayette is an iron-ore ghost

town which boomed from 1867 until 1892 when the demand decreased for its kind of iron. Here the kilns and ovens and casting house formed the molten metal into pig iron.

The road to Fayette meanders the length of the Garden Peninsula. The lighter woods of maple and birch give way to a darker jungle of pine. Along this road, as with many in the Upper Peninsula, the early spring of each year offers a delightful sight. Large herds of deer leave their winter retreats to nibble the tender grass at the roadsides. The frozen ground thaws here long before it relinquishes its hold deeper in the forest.

Fayette is on a tiny hook of land jutting into Big Bay De Noc. It falls away from the higher grounds of the Garden Peninsula so a ring of towering cliffs forms a majestic backdrop for the ghost town and state park. The founders of Fayette must have chosen the site for its beauty as well as its strategic bayside location.

To the north, on the sheltered side of Fayette's land hook, is Snail Shell Harbor. Thousands of tons of ore were shipped from here to the lower lake cities. Fayette's two smelting furnaces produced a high-quality charcoal iron; the town was the scene of a great deal of experimentation in early smelting processes.

The town site was acquired for a state park in 1959, and now the remains of the city are protected against further disintegration. Such structures as the machine shop, hotel and lime kiln still stand. Museums are open in the doctor's residence and the Opera House, and the salt-box house of the iron-works supervisor is decorated with period furnishings. The rest of the village can be seen in various stages of disrepair.

Hiawatha National Forest again joins the coast just before the Upper Peninsula bends southwest toward Wisconsin. Most of the campgrounds are on picturesque inland lakes surrounded by conifers and Northern hardwoods that attain blazing color in autumn. Only one picnic site, Peninsula Point, overlooks Lake Michigan. U.S. Route 2 leaves the lakefront to cut through this western segment of the forest; several foot and auto trails leave the highway to wind through the woods. Wildlife here is quite abundant. Black bear and deer are common, and moose have occasionally been sighted. Bald eagles reign in the most remote regions; rare sandhill cranes seek the marshes for a protected summer home.

J. W. Wells State Park, also in the Upper Peninsula, is a narrow strip of land on the Michigan side of Green Bay, twenty-three miles northeast of Menominee. Its three miles of sand beach plus the smallmouth bass and perch fishing in the bay make the park a popular summer resort. Wells is unique for its hog-back, a chain of irregular hills that was molded by passing glaciers. Foot trails lead to the ridge and through the woods and open glades of the park. They also lead to the park's frontage on the Big Cedar River.

Late-autumn trees are reflected in a quiet inland pool. The rustic farms of Door County's interior rival the charms of its wild coast and primitive forests.

Harmann Studios

A field of daisies carpets the ground at the foot of the lighthouse on tiny Cana Island near Jacksonport on the Lake Michigan side of the Door Peninsula.

Wisconsin's Door County Peninsula has an almost fabled beauty to the Great Lakes' residents. Thousands travel its seventy-five-mile-length each year. In its rocky cliffs and shards, the Door is reminiscent of Lake Superior's rugged coast; it is unique in Lake Michigan's generally sandy shore. The Door's unusual geography is due to its unusual geology.

Shallow pre-glacial seas deposited limestone here which hardened after the seas' demise. For 350 million years, erosion worked on the limestone, eking out one valley where Green Bay now is and another that became Lake Michigan. Glaciers badgered these valleys, enlarging them into the present bay and lake. But the solid limestone of the peninsula's spine resisted the icy digging.

The peninsula is the hard edge of the Niagara Escarpment; this extremely tough dolomite (one of the oldest formations on earth) arcs for nine hundred miles through Michigan and Canada to end in New York. There its rugged face supports the tumultuous waters of Niagara Falls. The glaciers could not break down the Door's dolomite back so they pushed over it, depositing a thin layer of gravel. Large granite boulders, called glacial erratics, are strewn over the ground. These dark rocks rest in stark contrast to the whitish dolomite cliffs of the Door's magnificent shore.

Four state parks protect large stretches of the Door Peninsula's lush pine and hardwood forest. Two of the parks have long been established; Newport, on the far north tip of the peninsula, has reached only the earliest stages of development. Rock Island State Park, an islet off the extreme end of the Door, is a remnant of true wilderness. It provides only for backpacking hikers and can be reached only by boat.

The site of a nineteenth-century logging village on Newport Bay is also the site of Newport State Park. Lilac bushes, cherry trees and cabin foundations are a reminder of the past. Old dock cribs in the bay recall the village's early fishing ventures; today, scuba divers seek sunken relics in the bay.

Most of Newport will be left as a natural wild area and development will be limited to the shore area. Its seven-mile shoreline has both a sand and gravel beach plus rugged rock cliffs. The hiking trails follow the vestiges of old logging trails, so few new slashes will be cut through the woods.

The park will remain primitive in an attempt to preserve its marshland. This delicate fen is the last near the lakeshore in Wisconsin. It spreads its reedy fingers of still water along the shore, supporting a self-sufficient little world of aquatic plants, insects, waterfowl and small mammals.

The Door's southernmost state park is Potawatomi, named for its earlier settlers. The park resides on the Green Bay side of the peninsula, just a few miles from the village of Sturgeon Bay. From the steep limestone slopes of Potawatomi's shore, the terrain lifts inland to a peak of 150 feet. Here a high observation tower presents a stunning panorama of the peninsula and bay.

Extremely thick pine forests carpet the rugged landscape, broken only by the intermittent shards of limestone outcroppings. Dozens of bird species fill these woods with a constant chatter.

Potawatomi is a year-round park. In the fall, its hardwoods are a brilliant tapestry against the blue bay waters. The winter draws skiers, tobogganists and snowmobilers. Spring coats the forest floor with a profusion of wildflowers, and the park goes to work in the summer, hosting thousands of campers and picnickers.

As the dolomite cliffs loom through the Potawatomi forest, so, too, do they dominate Peninsula State Park, the Door's largest preserve. Peninsula is named not for the Door, but for its own triangular grounds that jut into Green Bay between Fish Creek and Ephraim. Peninsula's seven-mile shore is a series of high bluffs; their foot is rimmed with a narrow cobblestone beach. Back from the shore, the cliffs rise to 180 feet under a densely wooded cover. Numerous overlooks along the scenic park drives offer charming views of the necklace of islands that rings the park's peninsula. In the summer, students from the University of Wisconsin present excellent shows, generally about Great Lakes life, in the park's amphitheater.

On the northernmost point in Peninsula State Park sits Eagle Lighthouse, which has supervised Green Bay ships for more than one hundred years. Green Bay has always been a risky waterway for mariners; early French explorers called the bay's tricky entrance *Porte des Morts*, Death's Door. Eagle Lighthouse is now automated, and a museum has been opened in what was once the living quarters.

Four state parks in such a small land area give credence to the peninsula's popularity, but all of the Door's charms are not confined in the park grounds. After the original pine was lumbered away, man replaced the forest with another kind of tree. Now the peninsula is a major apple and cherry growing center. Oceans of blossoms color the Door each spring. The rustic charm of its tiny villages recall an earlier day. Time is slower in the Door; it

An overcast autumn day frames an ancient farm house (above), abandoned years ago when the land proved too tough for the plow. From a high cliff in Peninsula State Park, (opposite), the scalloped coast outlines Green Bay.

is easy to forget a cluttered present with a visit to this lovely, clean land.

South along the shore toward Milwaukee, on the rim of Wisconsin's dairyland, the rolling terrain presents many bucolic scenes of green and golden fields sprinkled with neat little farm homes, capped silos and white-trimmed red barns. In the spring, dozens of red-wing blackbirds flicker between the field wildflowers. Often Lake Michigan's blue waters peek out behind the hills. A totally different sort of country from that which dominates the more northern lakeshore, it has, nonetheless, its own quiet beauty and easy-going appeal.

Point Beach State Forest, just north of Two Rivers, is a forest at work. At the southern end, a pine plantation has now produced acres of hardy young trees. To the north, hardwoods join the pine as the woodland blooms into a natural, near-wild stand. Contained along the shore by the farmland's open pastures, it is a remnant of the kind of woods more commonly found farther north. The forest

rises and dips over countless tiers of inland dunes that were pushed into place by a prehistoric sea.

The shoreline of Point Beach is wide and sandy, rising into rows of young low dunes. The park road bisects the forest for a shady, scenic drive. A beachhouse, picnic sites and campground near the shore make this the most popular part of the preserve. From here, hiking and nature trails meander over the dunes and away into the forest.

Terry Andrae — John M. Kohler State Park is a busy summer place; Milwaukeeans journey to it to escape for a weekend's camping. They scramble over Kohler's irregular dunes or meander the land's wide beach. Back from the shore, the hardwood and pine that can grasp nourishment from the sandy soil have stabilized the dunes and blossomed into a handsome, airy woodland.

Swimming is the most popular pastime at Andrae — Kohler. Unlike Superior, Lake Michigan

84

Linda B. Myers

From the observation tower in Potawatomi State Park (above), a panorama reveals the rolling land that yields to steep cliffs on Green Bay. Sand dunes, stabilized by beach grasses, lift inland (opposite) at Terry Andrae-John M. Kohler State Park.

warms to sixty degrees and above in the summer. The park's hiking and horse trails are open to snowmobilers in the winter. Terry Andrae has a lovely shady campground set back from the lake-front picnic sites and beach. Kohler is the newest addition to the Andrae — Kohler complex so it is still to be developed.

The same is true of Harrington Beach State Park. Its very underdevelopment, however, gives the park its hint of wild things. The woods push to the very edge of the beach; a small pond quietly awaits fishermen a little way inland. The damp mossy forest floor is a perfect haven for a lavish blanket of wildflowers.

Of Illinois' sixty miles of Lake Michigan shore, at least two-thirds belongs to Chicago and its satellite cities. So the Land of Lincoln can be forgiven for having only one state park on the waterfront; three and one-half miles of shore belong to Illinois Beach State Park.

This is an extremely hard-working park, hosting over a million visitors annually. It does not have the wild appeal of the North country, but in its very development, it offers a wide variety of pleasures to city-softened campers.

The park's wide beach is backed by a series of sand ridges; prevailing westerly winds perpetually drive the sands from the shore so Illinois Beach's dunes are small. A bit inland, they are stabilized by a covering of black oak and the rare shrub, Waukegan juniper. On the dry, shifting sands even prickly pear feels quite at home.

Beach houses, picnic grounds and a playground ring the shore; campgrounds and a new lodge offer modern accommodations to outdoor and indoor vacationers. Several foot trails dissect the park as does the slow-moving Dead River.

Illinois Beach offers two unusual varieties of trees. Along the river bank is a growth of Austrian and Scotch pines planted by Robert Douglas in 1860. The woods also harbor several fine specimens of Indian trail trees. Years ago, the Potawatomi marked their trails by bending limber saplings over to arc about four feet above the ground. The trees were fastened in this position, pointing in the direction of the trail. As the tree aged, the bend became permanent although the top continued to grow vertically. These twisted elms and oaks became lasting markers of the Indian routes.

Linda B. Myers

Between Gary and Michigan City, Indiana, a stretch of pre-glacial land has been given the protection it needs to continue in its ancient ways. In this prime industrial area, the land was in real danger. However, the Department of the Interior has lately become concerned with saving the nation's shorelines and with bringing more national lands within easy reach of America's highly populated areas. As a perfect combination of both goals, Indiana Dunes National Lakeshore was authorized in 1966 and dedicated in 1972. Land acquisition and development is underway. The state and Federal lands, now totaling over ten thousand acres of dunes and bogs, forests and beaches, are preserved in the busy center of American industry.

The enormous Indiana Dunes are storytellers of ancient days. They are the shores bulldozed by the ancient waters of a lake now called Lake Chicago.

This original lake was huge compared to its offspring, Lake Michigan. As it navigated various drainage areas for itself, Lake Chicago receded in stages; with each recession it left a beachline about twenty feet lower than the previous one. This receding shore became the ridges of sand dunes that run parallel to Lake Michigan and are visible for a full fifty miles inland.

Today, the dunes tower to over two hundred feet. Winds sweep down Lake Michigan, stirring the waters to wash even more sand onto the dunes, continually driving them inland. The dunes nearest

(continued on page 90)

Overleaf: *The lighthouse at Algoma, Wisconsin, rises above ground mists and frozen piers on a cold morning.*

87

the shore are unstable mounds; on a windy night you can hear the moving sand whispering in a low, muffled hum.

The moving dunes near shore are a natural windbreak for the ridges behind them. On the protected dunes, hardy beach grasses and spindly cottonwood can grasp a foothold. Drawing nourishment from the sandy ground, they grow and stabilize the dunes. Further inland, other vegetation like oak and hickory joins the pioneer plants until the dunes bloom into a full, diversified forest. Flora from the North and South mingle in Indiana Dunes National Lakeshore. Desert plants thrive on the sunny drifts where temperatures may soar over one hundred degrees; white pines rise to the cold north breezes on the shaded, windward slopes.

In the gullies between the dunes, the land gives way to marshy thickets and swamps. Here is yet another unique characteristic of Indiana Dunes National Lakeshore. Pinhook Bog is a true quaking bog that is a remnant of pre-glacial waters. It and Cowles Bog have remained in a nearly natural condition. Somehow they have made it through the centuries in an otherwise densely populated area of the country. Both bogs support a tremendous variety of wetland animal and plant life. Only limited access will be allowed to these marshes in hopes of keeping them as natural as they now are.

In fact, relatively little development will be made anywhere in Indiana Dunes National Lakeshore. Of the thirteen-and-one-half-mile beach, only the West Beach Unit, near Gary, will receive modern facilities. Beach houses and picnic grounds will accommodate daytime guests.

Inland, one more day-use unit will be developed where walking trails will lead to the old Bailly Homestead. Joseph Baille (the spelling changed some years later) was a French-Canadian who built a trading post near the Little Calumet River. He arrived in 1822, becoming northwest Indiana's first white settler. Several of the original buildings still survive and will soon be restored.

The only campgrounds in the area are under state management in Indiana Dunes State Park. This park, with three miles of frontage, is within the borders of the national lakeshore. It has ample beaches, trails and facilities; the state park will remain the dominant recreation grounds for the entire dune area.

S. Furushima

The overcast sky of a winter morning backlights frozen park benches and a single walker. Even in the Chicago parks solitude can occasionally be grasped.

A couple walks the beach at Indiana Dunes National Lakeshore. The unstable dunes near the lake are constantly trembling in the wind, diligently moving ever inland.

Rounding the southern end of the lake and heading north through Michigan again, an abundance of state parks stand out because of their sand dunes. The same ridges that are visible in Indiana appear along great stretches of the Lower Peninsula's western shore.

Holland and Warren Dunes state parks both have exceptionally large dunes. Those at Warren Dunes are both wooded and bare. Great Warren Dune, Tower Hill and Pikes Peak are sandy delights for would-be mountain climbers. Inland from the beach area is a two-hundred-acre virgin forest,

Warren Woods, which is being preserved in its natural condition as an ideal research forest.

Holland, a rather small park, is in the middle of spectacular lofty dunes. But the busy campground draws more than dune *aficionados*; it is also in the middle of tulip country. Holland, Michigan, is nationally renowned for its annual Tulip Time festival. Millions of multicolored blooms line every street, lawn and park. The little city even has a two-hundred-year-old, sixty-ton windmill, hauled all the way from Rotterdam to add to the old Dutch atmosphere.

Van Buren, P. J. Hoffmaster and Muskegon state parks all feature numerous scenic dunes. Although lower than those of Warren Dunes and Holland, they are not as bald. The dunes of these three parks have been stabilized by bright, airy woods.

Muskegon State Park, just outside the city of the same name, fronts on both Lake Michigan and

The shifting sand at Indiana Dunes has nearly buried a mature tree. The moving dune will eventually cover the entire tree before going elsewhere.

Ken Short

Muskegon Lake. The inland lake abounds in pike, bass and bluegill. This part of Michigan is near the southern boundary of the pine belt, and Muskegon's forest is an unusually dense and attractive pine and hardwood mix. There is a fine view from the top of an old reconstructed Block House, not far from the inland lake's shore, of this lush forest as it dips and rolls over the dunes to the beach of Lake Michigan.

The dunes of Silver Lake State Park, eight miles southwest of Hart, are very young. The Egyptian

pyramids pre-date them. Consequently, they are still drifting and bouncing along at the rate of about five feet per year. These shiny dunes can be reached only by trail, and thus are less crowded than the dunes of most Lake Michigan parks. From a point high amidst the lonely sands, the surroundings are reminiscent of an endless expanse of Arctic snow drifts.

A short hike inland is Silver Lake, the namesake of the park. It is ringed with a fine beach and the campground–picnic area is located near its shore.

Southwest Michigan's only lakefront state park that claims no dunes is also one of Michigan's busiest. One million visitors crowd Grand Haven State Park's forty-eight acres every year. It is small enough that almost all of the park is located on the broad, flat beach so very little shade protects its picnic and campgrounds from the hot summer sun. Due to its situation on the mouth of the Grand River, Grand Haven is a favorite camp of perch fishermen.

Within the village limits of Pentwater is a small strip of land donated by the family of Charles Mears, an early Michigan lumber baron and shipbuilder. A view from the top of the biggest dune, "Old Baldy," shows the surrounding dunes, beach and breakwater of Mears State Park. The little preserve has no woods to speak of, but it does offer every modern facility from bathhouse to boat launch.

Many of southwestern Michigan's state parks are so small that they have lost much of their wilderness appeal. Of course, their well-developed grounds provide much needed recreation areas for city-weary visitors. But for a larger forest and more wildlife than is usually seen in the southwest preserves, Ludington State Park is outstanding.

Ludington, on an elbow of land between Lake Michigan and Hamlin Lake, is a little more than midway up the Lower Peninsula — far enough north to support a dense woodland, far enough south to easily accommodate the more populated areas. Its nearly four thousand acres and relatively limited access have protected a dense forest of conifer and hardwood which, in turn, harbors deer, red fox and raccoons. Even a flock of Canada geese makes Ludington its year-round home. The forest floor buckles and dips over hills, ravines and low, stable dunes. Twenty-five miles of color-keyed trails crisscross the woods.

Hamlin Lake, created over a century ago by damming up its access to Lake Michigan, became an active waterway for the lumber boom, and a bustling logging town soon grew on its shores. In 1888, however, the Mill Dam burst and the entire village, plus a million feet of white pine logs, were swept into Lake Michigan. Only the remains of the mill and cemetery from the original village can still be seen in Ludington State Park. The dam has now been replaced, making Hamlin Lake Michigan's largest artificial lake.

Another reason why Ludington has retained something of its wilderness appeal lies to the north where the Lake Michigan Recreation Area of Manistee National Forest is located adjacent to it. Nearly 500,000 acres of woodland are scattered in patches of national protection. Once, following the logging and fires of the lumber era, this land looked like a big bald sand dune. Reclamation, begun in 1938, was a particularly difficult task, for the reluctant forest was not easily coaxed back to the sandy soil. A few scattered hollows still show the scars of blown-out areas.

For the most part, however, Manistee National Forest is once again a dark, lush growth. The only large sand area is the broad handsome beach of the Lake Michigan Recreation Area. The site is serviced by a campground at the mouth of Porter Creek.

Frothy, bubbling streams and rivers form a checkerboard of fresh waterways throughout the forest. The lovely and primitive Pere Marquette River is presently being considered for inclusion in the National Wild and Scenic Rivers System. Its clear waters cut deep into a wilderness so unspoiled that a visitor feels like the first *voyageur* to ever canoe its swift currents. Where this river empties into Lake Michigan, a cross-topped memorial marks where Father Marquette died in 1675.

About eight miles north of the Lake Michigan Recreation Area (and two miles north of Manistee, Michigan) is Orchard Beach State Park, where an airy woods of birch, oak and wild apple trees rim a high bluff overlooking the park's Lake Michigan beach. This bluff runs almost the full length of the grounds, affording Orchard Beach several of the lakeshore's most scenic vistas.

Sixty-four miles of Lake Michigan shore, thirty-three of it on islands, has recently come under the protection of Sleeping Bear Dunes National Lakeshore. The more than sixty thousand acres of the preserve also include fifteen inland lakes.

Long before the Federal Government established the Sleeping Bear preserve in 1970, the Chippewa established its history. According to their legend, a giant black bear and her two cubs began to swim the Great Water from Wisconsin to the Michigan wilderness. When the mother bear reached shore, she turned and realized her cubs had tired and lagged behind. So she settled down on the sandy

Richard Parks

94

*Far across the wide expanse of sandy shore,
a low sun (opposite) illuminates the steel mills at the
southern end of Lake Michigan. Like ancient Egyptian slaves
(above), the winds of Indiana Dunes National Lakeshore
craft their own variety of sand pyramid.*

shore to wait for them. But they never arrived. The Sleeping Bear waits there still, an enormous dune rising 164 feet above Lake Michigan. Her two cubs are now South and North Manitou islands, both part of the national lakeshore.

Sleeping Bear Dunes National Lakeshore includes five thousand acres of large active and stable dunes. The highest, north of Platte Bay, are the Empire Dunes. Sleeping Bear, namesake for the lakeshore, is the world's largest moving dune. High upon it are eerie stands of ghost forests. Their bleached skeletons are exposed where the shifting sands have covered living trees, then once again

blown free. The major acreage of the park is a handsome second-growth forest that backs the dune area. Oak and aspen stabilize the sandy land and, where the soil is richer, maple and beech fill out the woodland. This section of the park will be left in its natural state; very little development will open it to further human encroachment. Therefore, an abundance of wildlife roams the hidden places of the lakeshore.

North Manitou Island will remain primarily a primitive vacationland. Limited camping and beach facilities are now being planned. South Manitou, the smaller of the two, will become the most extensively developed. It supports a rich growth of virgin timber that the lumber barons miraculously missed. Tall white cedar more than five hundred years old dominates the Valley of

95

Ken Short

Tracing swirled patterns in the sand, sparse grasses (above) gain a tenuous foothold in Sleeping Bear Dunes National Lakeshore. Wind blew sand over cedars (right) then uncovered them, leaving their splintered fallen trunks looking like gray ghosts on the sand.

Giants. A deserted lighthouse, built on the island in 1871, will be restored as a marine museum. Presently, the easiest way to reach the islands is by the daily mail boat from Leeland.

Acquisition for Sleeping Bear Dunes National Lakeshore is just now underway. The grounds of D. H. Day State Park will be included; it is not yet decided whether Benzie State Park will be added. D. H. Day is in the heart of the prime dune section with ample wooded campgrounds, and these will be the major facilities for the national lakeshore. Benzie, with frontage on both Lake Michigan and the Platte River, is a large fishing park.

Sleeping Bear Dunes National Lakeshore is on the threshold of the "little finger" of the mitten-

shaped Lower Peninsula. This finger, Leelanau Peninsula, is bounded by Lake Michigan on one side and Grand Traverse Bay on the other. The Chippewa called this area the Land of Delight and, indeed, it is. Its one-hundred-mile shoreline is speckled with private resorts and little camps. Several quaint resort towns earn their living from the vacationers who trek to the forests, dunes, sand beaches and inland fishing lakes. High bluffs and ridges ring the peninsula, offering lofty lookouts over some of the state's most pleasing scenery. Leelanau Peninsula is more developed than most backpackers would enjoy, but for visitors who appreciate natural attractions as well as ample shopping and entertainment, this is a prime vacation region.

On the south end of the "little finger," at the inland tip of Grand Traverse Bay's West Arm, is the area's largest resort center, Traverse City. The community bustles all year but especially in mid-July when 400,000 visitors come to its National Cherry Festival, a joyous celebration of the region's harvest of 100 million pounds of tart red cherries. That is approximately one-third of all produced in the entire world.

Traverse City State Park, three miles to the east of town at the sandy head of the East Arm, is a hard-working little campground during the cherry festival. Even after the harvest is in, the park is the base camp for the multitude of attractions throughout the area. Not only is Leelanau Peninsula close by but the long, narrow Old Mission Peninsula (which cuts Grand Traverse Bay into its West and East arms) puts on a gorgeous color show every fall. Fishing, hiking, skiing, sightseeing are all part of the Land of Delight at Grand Traverse Bay.

Little Traverse Bay, less than twenty miles northeast of the mouth of Grand Traverse Bay, is an equally attractive vacation mecca. A bevy of inland lakes is this area's primary drawing card. Charlevoix, near the mouth of the bay, is a popular resort center for both cross-country traffic and Great Lakes boaters. From here, the ferry leaves daily — weather permitting — for Beaver Island.

At the head of Little Traverse Bay is Petoskey State Park, one of Michigan's newest. Its nearly three hundred acres offer extensive camping and day-use facilities; even a park naturalist is on duty

97

Fort Michilimackinac at Mackinaw City is one of the finest reconstructions in Great Lakes country. Excavation has revealed many artifacts from the eighteenth century.

to conduct evening interpretive programs. Petoskey has a fine sandy beach like all western Michigan state parks.

Well, almost all. The most notable holdout is Wilderness State Park, about twenty-five miles up the coast from Little Traverse Bay, where the beach is primarily composed of fine smooth pebbles. This spacious park, on the Straits of Mackinac and just about eight scenic miles west of Mackinaw City, is actually a seven-thousand-acre peninsula jutting west into Lake Michigan. To the north of it is Big Stone Bay, at the entrance of the straits. To the south is little Sturgeon Bay. The peninsula comes to an end at Waugoshance Point, with Waugoshance Island just offshore. The rocky coastline that surrounds Wilderness State Park is unique in western Michigan scenery.

Wilderness is just that. Its forest is so thick it is almost impenetrable. In many secluded spots, you

would swear that no man had set foot there before you. Only a few hiking trails wend their way through the lush growth.

Most of the development — camping, picnic grounds and beach — is on Big Stone Bay. The primeval forest backs up this clearing in the wilderness. A wildlife refuge hidden in the woods protects an abundance of deer, beaver and waterfowl. Wilderness State Park is one of the most delightful preserves on all of Lake Michigan.

If the Mackinac Bridge (see Chapter Seven) is designated as the arbitrary border between lakes Michigan and Huron, then Michilimackinac Historic State Park is an attraction of both, for the park grounds are located on both sides of the long bridge.

To the one side, the west, is the reconstruction of Fort Michilimackinac. Originally built in 1715 by the French, the fort became a busy *voyageur*

*The long Chicago to Mackinac sailing race
is an important and prestigious annual affair on
Lake Michigan, and lures sailors from
all over the country.*

supplied with all the goods, from flintlock pistols to barrels of rum, that would have been for sale or trade in the 1700's. The main museum is housed in the soldiers' barracks; here the artifacts of the digging are on display. Just outside the stockade is a collection of the embarrassingly cruel punishment devices used to keep the little community at Mackinac in strict order.

On the other side of the bridge, to the east, is the new Mackinac Maritime Park. Opened in 1972, usurping the land of a former campground, the park is only open during the day. Old Mackinac Point Lighthouse is the main attraction. It has been restored as a museum of the straits' marine history. Future plans for the park include the establishment of an eighteenth-century-type shipyard. Here, replicas of historic vessels will be built in public view.

From the wilds of its north shore to the industrial complex along the south, Lake Michigan gives everything a lake can give. It has not been as lucky as Superior to be situated far from the populated hub of America, so it has had to work much harder to fulfill what man has asked of it.

And man has asked a lot. But Lake Michigan has always met the request. It is truly the Great Water.

base for the fur trade. The British claimed the fort in 1761, but two years later the garrison there was massacred during the Pontiac War. It was soon reoccupied and remained an active post until 1781, when the British abandoned it for new fortifications on Mackinac Island.

Reconstruction on the fort began in 1959. The slow, careful work of the archeologists still goes on; visitors can watch the digging process and see each new artifact as it is unearthed.

The reconstruction is one of the most historically authentic anywhere in the United States. Excellent records guided the rebuilding. A twenty-foot-high, oak-pegged stockade rings the traders' homes, priest's and officers' houses, church and blacksmith shop. The King's storehouse has been

The North Channel of Lake Huron, separated from the main lake body by Manitoulin Island and numerous smaller islands, is a docile waterway with reedy shores and many islets.

Joe Kirkish

HURON
First Discovered, Least Known

Lake Huron, the first Great Lake discovered, is the second largest, the third in the lake chain, the fourth most populated, and the last to come to the American mind. Lake Superior is well known for its pristine beauty; lakes Michigan, Erie and Ontario are the backyard pools for millions of Americans. But Lake Huron is a stranger to all states but Michigan. The remainder, and greatest portion, of this lake is Canadian. It is integrally bound to the beginnings of Canada's history and its present lifestyle.

Lakes Huron and Michigan are the only two Great Lakes with the same water level. Their waves meet at the deep channel of the Straits of Mackinac. From here, Huron's whitecaps surge across 22,800 square miles to exit into Lake St. Clair and on to Lake Erie.

The only Americans to live by Lake Huron are Michiganders. The sites and parks they have set aside are many and varied. Especially well known are the attractions of the Straits of Mackinac.

Connecting Michigan's Lower and Upper peninsulas, between Mackinaw City and St. Ignace, is the lovely Mackinac Bridge. Its ivory towers are visible for miles from either side, piercing the clear blue Northern skies. This is one of the world's longest, costliest bridges and was one of the most difficult to construct. Its builder, David B. Steinman, had been told it was a bridge that could not be built. The violent winds and vicious currents of the straits battled the concept of being spanned. But Steinman succeeded and did his job well; the five-mile-long, four-lane-wide suspension bridge has been deemed one of the safest spans in the world. It has become a new Northwest Passage, replacing the hours of waiting for the now-gone ferries. Very few man-made structures can rival the natural grace and splendor of the bridge at Mackinac.

Visible from the bridge are several Lake Huron islands. The largest is Bois Blanc, pronounced "Bob-Low," which harbors Black Lake State Forest. Soldiers from Fort Mackinac used to come here for their firewood. Northwest of Bois Blanc is tiny Round Island, part of Hiawatha National Forest. Prior to the 1760's, Indians lived on the island; the only sign of white men's presence is an abandoned lighthouse, built in 1873. Round Island's profuse forest is being preserved in a natural wilderness condition.

With the exception of Niagara Falls, Mackinac Island is no doubt the best known site of the Great Lakes. This three-by-two-mile paradise has been a vacationland for a century. The earliest luxury steamers from ports on the lower lakes deposited their wealthy cargo of foreign dignitaries, government officials and the idle rich at the splendid Grand Hotel. The magnificent white monarch still reigns the island, its great pillared porch (some claim it is still the longest in the world) overlooking a myriad of flowers on a rolling lawn that sweeps to the clear water of the straits.

Long before the Grand Hotel called pleasure seekers to its lush gardens and palatial rooms, Mackinac Island called to the British. They built new fortifications, Fort Mackinac, here in 1781 when they became aware that Fort Michilimackinac on the mainland might be a great deal harder to defend. The stone ramparts, the officers' stone quarters and the south sally port still exist from the original structures. Today, the officers' stone quarters – the oldest surviving building in Michigan – contains displays of early-day period settings as well as a public tea room. The south sally port is an original fort entrance which is still used by visitors today. The remainder of the fort buildings are restored structures that were added in the nineteenth century. Each building, from the soldiers' barracks to the post hospital, is furnished in a manner which represents early Fort Mackinac life

style. The Mackinac Museum is housed in the officers' wooden quarters.

Mackinac Island radiates with the charm of bygone days. No motorized vehicles are allowed; instead, guests ride horses, rent buggies or bicycles, or simply walk the island's innumerable paths. There is a short airstrip on the island, but most visitors take the ferries from either Mackinaw City or St. Ignace.

The ferries arrive at the city of Mackinac Island which lies on the south shore, between its harbor and the high cliffs that sharply lift inland. Between the picturesque village and Fort Mackinac, higher in the hills, are the handsome gardens and memorial of Marquette Park.

The village grew in the 1780's as a fur trading post. Several sites, from a trader's home to fur warehouse, are reconstructed structures of John Jacob Astor's American Fur Company. Also restored is an Indian Dormitory which was built in 1838 to house up to four thousand Indians who came to do business with the island's U.S. Indian Agency. It is presently a museum of Indian artifacts.

While several of these ghosts from the past inhabit the city of Mackinac Island, the fur trade is gone. The village today lives on the tourists who flock to its gift shops, candy stores and restaurants. From its harbor, as from Fort Mackinac and the Grand Hotel, the view is a stunning panorama of the islands of the straits, the two peninsulas of Michigan, the Mackinac Bridge and the international shipping trade.

The backside of Mackinac Island, to the north, is still a forest with a lush carpet of mosses, lichens and wildflowers. A main trail circles the coast; from it, more secluded paths wind inland to various natural attractions. The best known of these is a land bridge called Arch Rock, which rises 146 feet above Lake Huron and spans about fifty feet. Another favorite formation is Sugar Loaf, a great limestone rock rising seventy-five feet over the surrounding island. Chippewa legend says it was so named because it used to be a gigantic bee hive with every crack caulked with rich, sweet honey. It was also one home of Manabozho, the spirit of Longfellow's *Song of Hiawatha.*

Besides the numerous natural attractions of the island's landscape are several man-made structures. An abandoned lime kiln (used by the British),

The Mackinac Bridge, known locally as Mighty Mac, ties together the two peninsulas of Michigan. It is one of the world's longest and most beautiful spans.

three cemeteries and restored Fort Holmes are all hidden away in the woods. They can be reached by hiking, biking or horseback riding the island trails.

Directly west of Mackinac Island, on the mainland near St. Ignace, is Straits State Park. The park is an excellent location for campers to venture out to the many surrounding attractions of Mackinac. Its high limestone bluff rises above the straits, overlooking the bridge, Mackinac Island and the Lower Peninsula. Along the waterfront, the beach is rocky and pockmarked with caves and sea stacks.

North of St. Ignace is the eastern section of Hiawatha National Forest. Beyond Straits State Park, picnickers can stop at a small recreation site called Foley Creek. Due to its heavy woods cover, the forest route around St. Martin Bay to the east is a favorite tour for seeing the colorful fall foliage.

Farther east is the beautiful island group known as Les Cheneaux. These islands were on the earliest *voyageur* and explorer route from Montreal to Mackinac. One of the group, Government Island, is the property of Hiawatha National Forest. The remains of an abandoned U.S. Coast Guard station plus two rustic picnic sites are the only breaks in the uninterrupted wilderness of the preserve.

The easternmost state park in Michigan's Upper Peninsula is four-hundred-acre De Tour State Park, near the Ontario border. Located on St. Vital Bay, it is only partially developed with limited camping facilities. There is a boat launch on the bay and a swimming beach near by.

Just east of De Tour is Drummond, one of Michigan's largest islands. It is in the chain of sizable Ontario islands that form the northern mouth of Georgian Bay. The Maxton Bay campground of the Munuscong State Forest is located on Drummond Island which can be reached by ferry from the Michigan mainland.

Georgian Bay is a great and gorgeous wash of crystalline blue waters, liberally sprinkled with a cluster of islands: islands of limestone shards from the Niagara Escarpment or granite outcroppings of the Pre-Cambrian Shield; islands from bald, windswept rocks to lush, pine jungles; islets so small that they disappear in high waters to Manitoulin, the largest freshwater island in the world.

The forty-eight thousand islands of Georgian Bay lure all sorts of mariners. Boat tours from mainland villages intertwine them; their harbors are rife with rich yachts and colorful sails. Among their bays and shoals, little boats trawl for the cold-water trout, whitefish and perch. Picnic grounds spot a fistful of islands that cluster near the mainland and sandy beaches rim a fistful more.

Michigan Tourist Council

The closest thing to motorized transportation on Mackinac Island is the horse-drawn carriage (above). The Chippewa believed the island's Sugar Loaf Rock (opposite) to be the wigwam of the spirit Manabozho.

Sunken schooners imprisoned in island reefs draw professional and amateur scuba divers. The hulk of LaSalle's *Griffin* is believed to be lurking near Russell Island, just off the Bruce Peninsula.

It is impossible to describe here all of the Georgian Bay islands. So just a few of special interest will be considered.

North and South Limestone islands total only 640 acres; you will not find them on many maps. They are approximately twenty air miles from Parry Sound, west of Killbear Point Provincial Park. They are the wild and isolated homeland for thousands of protected and rare birds. Caspian terns, herring and ring-billed gulls, double-crested cormorants and great blue herons all nest here. Dozens of other species are frequent visitors. They are all at ease on these lonely islands, humanly inaccessible except in very calm weather.

Their limestone rock gave them their names. Imprinted in the smoother slabs are the fossils of a variety of sea life preserved from the Ordovician

The splendid Grand Hotel (above), built in 1887, stretches its porch 880 feet along a Mackinac Island bluff. Denying the forest floor total darkness (opposite), sun rays burst through the trees.

Period, 375 million years ago. Also extant is evidence of a long-ago Indian camp. The lonely Limestones will probably be deemed a wilderness area to protect them forever for the wild things.

Separating Lake Huron from Georgian Bay and the North Channel is Manitoulin Island, one hundred miles long and fifty miles wide.

At least three thousand years ago, the island was home for Indian ancestors; artifacts are on display in the museum at Little Current, the island's largest town. Three hundred years in the past, Chippewa roamed Manitoulin's forests and shores. Then, in the eighteenth century, *voyageurs* frequented the Hudson's Bay Company post at the present site of Little Current.

Manitoulin today has turned from the fur trade to the tourist trade. It has over one hundred inland

lakes, wide sandy beaches and a variety of resort towns. Eighteen tribes from six Indian reserves on Manitoulin exhibit their handicrafts, tribal dances and traditional ceremonies in an annual Pow Wow every August.

Manitoulin's south shore can be reached by the three-hour ferry ride from Tobermory on the Bruce Peninsula. From the north, a series of causeways and bridges connect it to the mainland.

To reach Manitoulin, the northern causeway crosses Great Cloche Island. Here, two sites figure strongly in ancient Indian life style. Legend has it that Dreamer's Rock was inhabited by a spirit who could tell the future. But he would only reveal it to those young braves who would fast and then sleep on the rock's rugged summit. Bell Rocks, a group

106

(continued on page 109)

H. Michael Brauer

H. Michael Brauer

of glacial boulders, were used by the Chippewa as a warning alarm. When struck by stones, Bell Rocks resounded in deep, ringing tones.

Not many national parks have to be reached by boat but such is the case at Georgian Bay Islands National Park. It is comprised of fifty islands, or parts of islands, that lie scattered like emerald beads along forty miles of southeastern Georgian Bay, from Macey Bay to Moose Deep Point, and, in addition, a small strip of mainland. Park lands also include 495-acre Flowerpot Island, a hundred miles to the northwest and four miles off the tip of the Bruce Peninsula.

Georgian Bay Islands National Park combines two distinct geological formations. The eastern islands are glacier-polished bedrock of the Pre-Cambrian Shield; Flowerpot Island to the west is hard limestone of the Niagara Escarpment. These islands were once the tops of hills; the channels between them were valleys.

Erosion has caused the peculiar caves and columns of the western island. The "flowerpots" are inventions of irrepressible waves which have eaten away the shoreline into tall pillars. The more durable rock at the tops of the stacks is better preserved and often broader than the wave-badgered rock at the bases. Early Indians found this strange and eerie island a taboo land to be avoided.

Indians did, however, visit Beausoleil, the largest island in the national park. It is believed that the Huron, during their flight from the Iroquois, hid their valuables on the island. The east shore area called Treasure Pits may contain these long-buried artifacts. The graveyard and village remains of a more recent nineteenth-century settlement are plainly visible.

Here, too, Champlain must have camped in 1615, when he first found Lake Huron, his Sweet-Water Sea. It would have been simple to beach a canoe on Beausoleil's long, sloping shore; the island's fat deer herd would have filled the crew's bellies. Even today, an abundance of wild-life from shrews and voles to beaver and deer inhabit the island. Inland marshes harbor a wide variety of water creatures. The shy and very rare massasauga rattlesnake finds a final refuge in the tall reeds.

At its northern tip, Lake Huron, through its North Channel, is just a few miles from Lake Superior and they share many characteristics, from bleak winters to cold, clean water.

The eastern islands of Georgian Bay Islands National Park are accessible by boat from mainland villages like Midland and Penetanguishene. Tours from Tobermory on the Bruce Peninsula visit Flowerpot Island. The only really modern campground in the park is located on the mainland, but docking facilities, primitive camps, picnic sites and trails are available on Beausoleil as well as on many of the smaller islands.

The Georgian Bay mainland is no less spectacular than its islands. It was called by the Huron *Ouendake*, "One Land Apart," and early Europeans referred to it as a fresh new world. It still is.

The Georgian Bay region was not settled until the mid-1800's when the railroads pushed north to Collingwood on the southern tip of the bay, and hardy pioneers eked out homesteads near the tracks. But the rugged, tough lands discouraged most, so northern Georgian Bay still has large wild tracts. To the north, fishing and lumber villages ring the bay; the southern towns are mostly resort and small manufacturing centers.

The solid granite of the Pre-Cambrian Shield formed the northeastern mainland as it did the islands. A jumble of shoals, cliffs, coves and shards mingle with thousands of lakes, rivers and streams. Where it can grab nourishment from the rock-bound terrain, lush wild forest claims the country. A large sector of mainland is considered a recreation reserve, and it is among the finest canoe regions in the world. Hundreds of routes cross the white water, portages and calms of innumerable waterways. The bayside is also excellent turf for rockhounds because a wide variety of stones were deposited here by retreating glaciers.

Farther down the bay, the Pre-Cambrian Shield gives way to the Niagara Escarpment. Ringing the south end are the "Blue Mountains" of the escarpment. A fine winter sports area, the mountains have helped bayside villages like Collingwood become year-round resorts. Summers fill their sandy beaches which replace the rockbound coast of the north.

On the mainland at the northern tip of the bay, where North Channel connects with the bay, is Killarney Provincial Park. Until recently, this enormous, 132-square-mile preserve was a natural environmental park meant to reserve the unique characteristics of the landscape. In 1971, it was deemed a primitive provincial park in order to promote total preservation. The present development is now being reversed. Roads are being closed, timbering is to be halted, the modern campground will be phased out. Only rustic sites will remain to accommodate experienced hikers

Gore Bay lies far below East Bluff (above) on Manitoulin, the Great Lakes' largest island. A young bicyclist (right) stops at reedy Lake George in the St. Mary's River, which connects Lake Huron with Lake Superior.

and present day *voyageurs*. Killarney is the only primitive park within relatively easy access of the populated lands of southern Ontario.

Killarney Provincial Park contains the heartland of the La Cloche Mountains. This lovely range rises to 1,700 feet through some of the last original white pine forest in North America. Viewed from the distance, its bald, white quartzite crests appear to be snow-coated peaks.

A smattering of clear rock-locked lakes dominate the La Cloche range. In the park, lovely inland Lake George is more accessible than the rugged Georgian Bay shore. O.S.A. Lake, named in honor of the Ontario Society of Artists, is another popular site. The wilds of Killarney Provincial Park inspired an entire school of well-loved Canadian artists known as the Group of Seven.

Sturgeon Bay Provincial Park is a small recreation provincial park on its own inlet, just about thirty miles north of Parry Sound. Almost all of the park is campground although a marsh rims its northern border. Its tiny sheltered bay makes it an excellent spot for fishing, boating and water sports. Sturgeon Bay is one of the few recreation parks with almost no daytime use facilities; to enjoy it, stop for the night.

About halfway down the eastern shore of Georgian Bay, north of Franklin Island and on the south tip of Shawanaga Bay, is a most unique rock outcropping. The formation, especially viewed from the bay, looks remarkably like a turtle. According to legend, the Sacred Turtle has the magical power to control the rough waters and violent winds of Shawanaga Bay. For hundreds of

years, Indians placed offerings of tobacco, coins or maple sugar before the turtle. If the god was pleased, it would calm the waters so the Indians could paddle across the bay safely. The Sacred Turtle guards the bay today as it has for centuries.

Not far from the watchful turtle, twenty-two miles northwest of Parry Sound, is Killbear Point Provincial Park. The three-thousand-acre natural environment park is one of Georgian Bay's most popular due to numerous trails, interpretive programs and golden beaches. Where the shore of Killbear's peninsula is not sand, it rises to sheer rocky cliffs. No snowmobiles are allowed in the park because it is a wintering area for deer.

Hundreds of beech trees in Killbear are engraved with bear tracks. Rows of four or five short dark grooves in the bark are the claw marks made several autumns ago when black bears climbed to feast on the trees' tender seeds. The south range of the bear and the north range of the beech overlap by only a few miles so the claw marks are not common.

Near Killbear are the skeletal remains of an early nineteenth-century trading post. The structures were burned long ago but their stonework is largely intact. Artifacts from the site are on display at the Royal Ontario Museum.

The roughly triangular land between southeast Georgian Bay and wind-ruffled lakes Simcoe and Couchiching is the ground known as Huronia. This land of the Huron is the cradle of Ontario history; Etienne Brulé visited it as early as 1610. Here have been found the earliest Indian, missionary and explorer artifacts.

111

The history of this small bit of Georgian Bay is still living in Midland. Near the town is a three-acre reconstruction of Sainte-Marie-Among-the-Hurons, the Jesuit mission and community that existed here in 1639. Within the palisades are such buildings as craftsmen's shops, the Jesuit Chapel and the Church of St. Joseph. The church protects the grave of St. Jean de Brebeuf, the missionary who was tortured and burned at the stake by the Iroquois in 1649. In the same year, the fathers burned their settlement so it would not fall into Iroquois hands. On a hill overlooking the reconstruction is the Martyrs' Shrine which honors the eight devout Jesuits at Ste-Marie.

Inside Midland, in Little Lake Park, is a full scale replica of a seventeenth-century Huron village. Within the settlement's palisades are the bark-roofed, long houses typical of early Huron life style. Artifacts of their culture are displayed in the village's museum.

On the east shore of Nottawasaga Bay, at the bottom of Georgian Bay, is Ontario's answer to Daytona Beach. Wasaga Beach is the longest freshwater beach in the world and a prime section of the seven golden miles is the shore of Wasaga Beach Provincial Park.

Wasaga has long been a vacation mecca. In fact, prehistoric Indians visited it thousands of years ago. They came seasonally to pick berries or hunt deer or take sturgeon that spawned in the Nottawasaga River. No tribes settled permanently on Wasaga's infertile dunes.

When the railroad passed this way in the mid-1800's, sun worshippers flocked to the beach in their coverall bathing suits. By the early 1900's, Model A's lined the beach while their wealthy owners frolicked in the gentle waves.

In Wasaga Provincial Park, on a small island in the Nottawasaga River, is the fascinating Museum of the Upper Lakes. The islet was formed by silt that settled around the hull of the HMS Nancy. The Americans sank this British schooner, a supply ship to Fort Michilimackinac, during the War of 1812. It has been raised and now rests in front of the museum on the island of its own creation.

Only fifteen miles west of Wasaga Beach is another small recreation provincial park primarily for campers. Craigleith Provincial Park is on the Niagara Escarpment; its level limestone shore is rife with fossils from the Ordovician Period. An exhibit center in the park identifies each form of sea life fossilized in the tough rock. The Blue Mountains form a picturesque backdrop for the popular park.

Georgian Bay is framed on the southwest by an appropriately lovely entranceway. The Bruce Peninsula is as charming as Lake Michigan's Door County. The shores of the peninsula, with the blue-green waters of Lake Huron to the west and Georgian Bay to the east, are alternately rocky cliffs and white sand beach.

Inland, the Bruce has the greatest variety of wildflowers in all of Ontario. A myriad of little rivers gurgle through rapids and falls throughout the peninsula. The tough spine of the Bruce is the Niagara Escarpment and it offers some of the

The Au Sable River winds through Huron National Forest. Following it and adjacent streams, a canoeist can paddle completely across Michigan from Lake Huron to Lake Michigan.

peninsula's most appealing scenery. To see it you must walk, and the Bruce Peninsula is the most arduous sector of the Bruce Trail. This 480-mile hiking trail, completed in 1967, cuts through the most heavily populated area of Ontario yet it manages to circumvent civilization throughout its entire length. The trail begins near Niagara Falls and wends all the way to Tobermory, the picturesque fishing village at the tip of the Bruce. Here

An endangered species nesting only in Michigan, this Kirtland's warbler is one of about a thousand left in the world. The birds require jack pines in burned-over areas to nest, and Huron National Forest provides this habitat.

scuba divers gather to investigate the many sunken ships in the brilliant waters of Georgian Bay.

Just six miles from Tobermory is Cyprus Lake Provincial Park. The sizable natural environment park graces the ninety-foot limestone cliffs overlooking the bay. The campgrounds and swimming beach are inland on Cyprus Lake; several little lakes in the park are linked by walking trails. Other trails lead through the balsam and cedar forest to the lofty lookout sites on Georgian Bay.

The Blue Water Highway skirts the Ontario coast from the tip of the Bruce to Sarnia, at the very southern end of Lake Huron. The shore is nearly all sand here where it greets the clean cool waters that have swept the entire length of Lake Huron. The 250 miles of gold and white sand are frequently backed by both bald and forested dunes. Four provincial parks take advantage of this sandy kingdom.

Inverhuron and Pinery provincial parks are both natural environment parks with long beaches slop-

ing gently into the lake; the shallow waters of Lake Huron's eastern shore make a fine splashing pool for young children. Both parks have good camps, extensive nature trails and excellent fishing. The stream that meanders through Inverhuron is stocked with brook trout; the Ausable River where it runs through Pinery is a natural fishing and canoe route.

Pinery's sandy dunes are topped with a fine oak, birch and pine forest that harbors a variety of wildlife from deer to ruffed grouse. The irregular terrain provides for winter skiing and tobogganing. Near the slopes are a skating rink and almost thirty miles of snowmobile trails. In warmer weather, the park overflows with the tourist trade from nearby

(continued on page 116)

Overleaf: Seen from Fort Mackinac, the Mackinac Island marina spreads out before Marquette Park. Bois Blanc Island is in the background.

113

Herman Ellis

114

Grand Bend, a bustling resort with a summer-long amusement park atmosphere.

Inverhuron was named for a lumbering village that existed about seventy years ago. The scattered remains of homesteads and a gristmill are left to tell the story, as is a small pioneer cemetery. Long before the loggers arrived, the Iroquois camped in Inverhuron's forest.

Point Farms and Ipperwash are recreation provincial parks geared to heavy daytime and camping use. Both are on the busy southeast coast of Lake Huron; a constant parade of multicolored sails dot the horizon before the parks' shorelines.

The rocky shore of Point Farms (named for western Ontario's first resort that existed in the 1860's on what is now park grounds) must be reached by steps that descend the seventy-five-foot-high clay banks that rim the park. Ipperwash, too, has a rocky raised coast where Duffus Creek runs to Lake Huron. But on either side of the short ridge are fine sandy beaches. Ipperwash was established in 1938, one of only eight Ontario provincial parks to exist before 1954.

Just about thirty miles southwest of Ipperwash, the Blue Water Bridge passes over the St. Clair River from Sarnia, Ontario, to Port Huron, Michigan. Michigan continues Ontario's efforts in reserving public lands along the south shore – Lakeport State Park is just ten miles north of the bridge.

The light breezes blowing across Lake Huron cool the sandy mile of Lakeport frontage. In back of the beach, running the length of the shore, a low bluff rises to some twenty feet. Perched here, near lovely stands of birch and oak, lawn-chair captains can oversee the continuous parade of Great Lakes freighters, polished yachts and bobbling sailboats as they ply to and from the St. Clair River.

The lake winds also ruffle the sands of Sanilac State Park, just north of Richmondville. Like Lakeport, Sanilac overlooks the shipping highway a few miles offshore. This 117-acre state park is still to be developed; relatively few campsites are available at the present time.

Port Crescent State Park is located on the tip of the thumb (Michigan's Lower Peninsula looks remarkably like a mitten). The park is bordered on the west by the Pinnebog River and its shore slopes to the resort-studded Saginaw Bay. The bay area was the heartland of Michigan's earliest lumbering.

A campground is at Port Crescent's east end. Most of the rest is two hundred acres of sand; a busy, wide beach is backed by low, rolling dunes. The farther inland you track the nature trails, the

denser grows the forest. Port Crescent bustles year round – summer's paths become winter's snowmobile trails.

Port Crescent's next-door neighbor is Albert E. Sleeper State Park. Only fifteen miles of U.S. Highway 25 separates their grounds. If Port Crescent is on the tip of the thumb, then Sleeper is on what you might call the thumbprint. It is a large, 963-acre, full-service state park, its beach sweeping back into the low round dunes that are typical of this part of Lake Huron. The calm waters of Saginaw Bay lure fishermen and boaters alike; Sleeper sponsors a boat rental service. Many trails traverse the dunes and woods if you care for a private stroll. Or tag along with the park naturalist

Ontario Ministry of Industry and Tourism

Flower Pot Island in Canada's Georgian Bay Islands National Park is a limestone promontory of the Niagara Escarpment. Waves have eroded its shore into top-heavy pillars (opposite), giving the island its name. An aerial view (above) reveals the rugged terrain.

on his guided hikes. Sleeper is still heavily forested as are many large tracts of the scenic thumb country.

A handsome park at the southwest end of the bay is the host beach for Bay City, Saginaw and Midland. So the extra long, extra wide beach of Bay City State Park is an industrious community sandbox. Likewise, its campground is a mecca for anglers who take on the pike, perch and sunfish of Saginaw Bay. Because of the heavy usage of Bay City State Park, a pleasant, little nature museum has been constructed. And despite its heavy usage, the forest still remains ample, cool and clean.

A narrow point of land descends into the blue waters of northern Saginaw Bay and bends slightly inland. On its sheltered side, this sandy hook forms Tawas Bay, an inlet known for its excellent fishing as early as the 1850's. In the earliest lumbering days, logs were hauled from miles around to the

mills that ringed the bay. Today the mills have given way to homes, resorts, campgrounds and Tawas Point State Park.

All of the land hook is within the state park grounds. Due to its unique shape, Tawas Point offers a two-mile-long sand beach. To the east, it faces the open waters and shipping lanes of Lake Huron; to the west are the little boats and gentler waves of Tawas Bay.

Tawas Point State Park receives some help in maintaining semi-wilderness environs because just north of it is Huron National Forest. While most of the 415,000 acres are inland, a corner of the forest extends to Lake Huron in the Tuttle Marsh Wildlife Area, a special sector that the forest service manages primarily for wildlife.

The highway skirts the shoreline of the wildlife area between East Tawas and Au Sable. There are no campgrounds here; they are all on the forest's

*The Lumberman's Monument (above) overlooks the Au
Sable River in Huron National Forest. The north shore of Lake
Huron (right) is a quiet semi-wilderness; south of it the Georgian
Bay Islands stretch across the lake like an emerald necklace.*

rivers, inland lakes and streams. Throughout the
Tuttle Marsh area, waterholes have been opened
and food patches cleared to support all manners of
Northern wildlife. Part of the forest's large annual
timber harvest comes from the woodlands around
Tuttle Marsh. Seeding and planting continuously
balance the extent of the cutting.

Over 650 miles of rivers and streams in Huron
National Forest make it one of Michigan's finest
canoe areas. One water route, dubbed the Shore-
to-Shore Trail, traverses the 220 miles from Lake
Huron to Lake Michigan. Or, if you prefer to hoof
it, forest trails follow a similar route.

The Shore-to-Shore Trail passes near the unique
Kirtland's Warbler Management Area. The Kirtland's warbler is an extremely rare song bird; only
about one thousand are left in the world. They
nest only in this area of Michigan and their scarcity

is due, in part, to their unusual nesting habits.
They require a forest fire now and then because
they nest only in the young jack pines that grow in
recently burned-over areas. Therefore, the management area undergoes carefully controlled, peri-
odic prescribed burning to maintain a homeland
for these charming little songsters.

Not far north of Huron National Forest a range
of hills begins to build high over Lake Huron. The
shoreline drive dips and rolls through them, offering stunning panoramas of the dense woodlands
and the blue Great Lake where it spreads out
below. This is the setting for Harrisville State Park.

Nestled in the hilly terrain, about thirty miles
south of Alpena, Harrisville is a particularly handsome park. Its woods are lush, its campgrounds
shady and its beach of fine, white sand. Like the
parks farther south on the Lake Huron shore,

Harrisville is an excellent grandstand for the foreign and domestic freighters silently cruising toward Great Lake ports. From when the hazy sun peeks over the morning lake until the fat moon rises at night, Harrisville is a photographer's joy.

No less endearing are the picturesque dunes of P. H. Hoeft State Park, farther to the north. The sandy mounds are backed by a series of ridges and broken bluffs, formed by ancient lake levels, which gives Hoeft its rugged landscape. This upper tableland, studded with rich pine and hardwood, overlooks the sloping sand beach far below. Because it is a large state park, a great many trails lead through its dunes into lonely forest places. You can still find a solitary retreat in Hoeft.

Only one more state park remains before the circuit of Lake Huron back to the Straits of Mackinac is complete. Cheboygan State Park is about twenty miles from the Straits on sandy Duncan Bay, directly south of Bois Blanc Island. Its club-shaped peninsula borders both the bay and Lake Huron. The park is well over nine hundred woodsy acres and will soon be one of Michigan's most modern preserves. It is still only partially developed although some campsites are available. And the lovely beach on docile Duncan Bay awaits the summer crowds that flock to the cool shores of northern Lake Huron.

Lake Huron — founded when Champlain thought he was on his way to Cathay in 1615; smaller only than enormous Superior; more isolated than any but lonely Superior; and maybe the last you think about. But ask the one who knows it — the one who has seen its green islands and climbed its gentle dunes. He can tell you Lake Huron's story because he knows its worth.

ERIE

Always fretful, always threatening, Erie is a moody lake. Its name, a corruption of the Iroquois word *erige*, means cat (the earliest French explorers called it *Lac Du Chat*, Lake of the Cat). Like a cat, the lake is undependable, independent. It does what it wants and when. The other Great Lakes can be calm and Erie will be furiously pulsing in a wild storm that has barreled down from the Canadian wilds. The others give some warning of impending gloom; Erie is so shallow (a mean depth of only ninety feet) it can raise to a tempestuous gale in a matter of minutes. Boaters are wary of it and even those who swim its shallows keep an eye to gathering clouds.

It offers man troubles beyond bad weather because Lake Erie seems to want to be a swamp — its restless shores collapse and chunks of good farmland fill in the lake basin. Its harbors must be dredged to keep them open and, in fact, most of them did not exist at all until men dug Erie a new coastline.

While the silty clay shores make it a quicksilver lake, they also account for one of Erie's most unique and delightful aspects. Especially to the west, the weak banks are spongy marshlands. Bulrushes, cattails and lilies infest the quiet pools along the lakeshore. Insects dart between the willowy reeds, erratic targets for fish and frogs from beneath and swooping waterfowl from above. This abundance of insects and aquatic plants has made the shoreline of Lake Erie one of North America's finest observatories for birds.

The fourth largest Great Lake, little Erie is less than half the size of Lake Michigan. It is the southernmost of the lakes so its surrounding flora at times has an almost tropical flavor. While its southern shore is an enormous industrial complex of Toledo, Sandusky, Cleveland, Erie and Buffalo, its northern shore has relatively few sizable communities. On the Canadian side, Lake Erie's coast is relatively smooth so very few good harbors offer footholds for lakeside settlements.

What the province of Ontario lacks in urban development, it more than recaptures in rural charm. The club-shaped land that extends between lakes Huron and Erie, encircling Lake St. Clair, has been called Ontario's Sun Parlor. This is a fertile greenhouse, an ambrosia of orchards and grain fields and vegetable gardens. The languorous summers gently coax weighty harvests of corpulent tomatoes and golden corn. The Sun Parlor feeds Ontario (as well as a large part of the rest of Canada) and has all the rustic charm of the Wisconsin farmlands.

This rolling country is the rich backyard of Amherstburg, on the Detroit River just north of its Lake Erie mouth. The quiet village retains the quaint narrow streets and Old-World homes that grew here over a century ago. It is the site of Fort Malden National Historic Park.

(continued on page 123)

Serene and tranquil now at the end of a day, Lake Erie is the perfect picture of a placid, friendly lake. But it is a hoax; wild storms can stir the shallow waters into a frenzy in a very few minutes.

Lake of the Cat

H. Michael Brauer

Olive Glasgow

The unmolested marshlands of Lake Erie (above) support many varieties of Northern swamp life. Glacial grooves on Kelleys Island (opposite) recall the Ice Age that gouged ruts six feet deep into the island's limestone.

Fort Malden was built by the British in 1797; at the same time, they laid out the town site of Amherstburg. The fort was needed to keep an eye on the Yankees at Detroit, and it played a major role in several battles during the War of 1812. Today, the fort contains the original earthworks and a few buildings; two of the structures house a museum devoted to fort history and artifacts. No armies have advanced for a hundred years, but Fort Malden still stands guard. It rests on the bank of the Detroit River, overseeing the great ships that quietly pass it by.

On a journey to Fort Malden, many travelers visit Holiday Beach Provincial Park, less than ten miles further down the Detroit where it broadens into Lake Erie. Holiday Beach is not so much a wilderness as it is a lakeside resort for Windsor, Ontario, just twenty-eight miles to the north. In many ways, it resembles a well-trimmed city park; its large, grassy recreation fields for sports like baseball and soccer are sprayed against insects, its fish pond is stocked with trout and its Lake Erie beach is cleaned of fish and debris daily. In the swamp, Bog Creek Marsh, at the park's northwest boundary, a relatively unmolested collection of aquatic insects flicker and dart before the waterfowl in pursuit.

Americans tend to forget just how diversified Canada is. The common image is of a huge country, stretching from the Arctic halfway to the Equator, that is one big ice-bound plantation of pine trees. Not so. In fact, several tracts of Canada's Lake Erie shore are almost tropical.

Point Pelee National Park, thirty miles southeast of Windsor, is as far south as northern California. It drops down on a golf-tee-shaped peninsula, the southernmost tip of the Canadian mainland. The mild climate of the low latitude is further tempered by the surrounding waters of Lake Erie.

Ohio Department of Natural Resources

Olive Glasgow

124

There are almost no pine trees at Point Pelee. Instead, the long hot summers cultivate a variety of plants that are found nowhere else in Canada. In the 3,500-acre park is one of the last small remnants of North America's original deciduous forest. The rare black walnut, sycamore, white sassafras and shagbark hickory sway above tangled drapes of grape vines and Virginia creeper. Clustered near their roots are southland shrubs like spicebush, swamp mallow and hop tree. Even the lemon-yellow flowers of the squat prickly-pear cactus brighten the ground when it is baked dry by the hot July sun. Coyotes and deer roam throughout the woodland.

Inland, Point Pelee is one of the last closed freshwater marshes on the continent. Its 2,500 acres of reed-choked pools hide muskrat and mink and breed swarms of water flies. About ninety different species of birds nest in and around the fen. A boardwalk traverses two-thirds of a mile of the marsh, ending at a twenty-foot tower.

As magnificent as this rare marsh and its deciduous forest are, they are not what most visitors come to see. Point Pelee is in the heart of two major bird migration flyways. In the spring (mid-March through the end of May) and in the fall (August through October) hundreds of thousands of warblers, blue jays, blackbirds, hawks and terns cross Point Pelee. The tip of the peninsula, known as the Point, is a long sand spit where watchers get the best view of the noisy and colorful flocks winging by.

Almost as spectacular as the bird migration is the autumn flight of dragonflies and wasps. At times, each tree and every shrub is coated with orange when the migrating monarch butterflies pause to rest on their long trip south.

The unique ground cover that attracts birds to Point Pelee is as delicate as it is rare. Consequently, no camping and few trails are offered but picnic sites dot the fourteen miles of sand beach. Automobiles are not allowed out on the sandy bird-watching area; instead a trackless, pollution-free train runs to the Point. An active naturalist project presents conducted hikes and special programs to explain fully the geology and geography of fragile Point Pelee National Park.

Visitors to Point Pelee find nearby Wheatley Provincial Park (less than ten miles to the northeast) a convenient place to spend the night. Wheatley is an excellent place to get a good close-up look at a marsh. It is primarily a still lagoon formed by the slow waters of Sugar and Boosey creeks and ringed by a forest of beech, cherry, walnut and dogwood. Once again, this woodland is unique in a country known for its Northern pine. Walkways cross the bogs to connect the mile-long sand beach on Lake Erie with the inland camp-grounds.

Hosts of songbirds flit from tulip trees to hickories to sassafras in the lush forest of Rondeau Provincial Park, forty miles northeast of Point Pelee. Mosquitoes and dragonflies govern the interior, as much marsh as it is dry land. A hike in this enormous natural environment park, the largest on Lake Erie, is reminiscent of what it must have been like to stroll centuries ago the primeval woods of the Carolinas.

Rondeau Provincial Park, five miles south of the little village of Morpeth, was established in 1894, making it Ontario's second oldest provincial park. It is on its own peninsula, which is shaped something like a teardrop, forming quiet Rondeau Bay on the west. This is the wilder side of the park where the fishing is good and labeled trails dissect the forest. To the east are the sandy beaches, picnic sites and camps along the Lake Erie shore. Here, too, is a museum devoted to the area's natural history.

Like Rondeau, Long Point Provincial Park is a marvelous observation center for migrating birds. Also like Rondeau, it is a large park on its own peninsula but it is not nearly so wild. Long Point, a recreation provincial park about eighty miles east of Rondeau, receives intense use all summer and into the fall. The smooth southern side of the long, narrow point (hence, its name) is an excellent sandy beach, one of Lake Erie's finest. The northern side, forming Long Point Bay, is an irregular coast laced with a sprinkling of tiny islands. The weedy waters of the islets and dipping shoreline harbor some of the best bass fishing left on Lake Erie. A boat ramp, ample campgrounds and picnic sites run down the spine of the Long Point peninsula, servicing swimmers to the lake side and fishermen to the bay.

On the eighty-mile coastline between Rondeau and Long Point are three more provincial parks. Port Bruce and Iroquois Beach are both recreation parks with excellent beaches and picnic facilities.

An immature red-tailed hawk patrols lake marshes for negligent mice and birds. Its predatory practices help maintain the fragile ecological balance of the wetland habitat.

H. Michael Brauer

*Sheathed in dew, a freshly engineered web (above) glitters
in the early morning sun. A popular pastime at Holiday Beach Provincial
Park (opposite) is skipping stones on the waters of Lake Erie.*

John E. Pearce is the only natural reserve provincial park on Lake Erie; it is more for nature study than public amusement although it does offer a few picnic sites.

The 782-acre wart of land that forms the eastern side of Long Point Bay is a natural environment provincial park called Turkey Point. Its first campers were Sulpician missionaries who visited the point as early as the 1670's and in 1795, Colonel John Graves Simcoe, the first governor of Upper Canada, planned the town site of a village, Charlotteville, that never grew. Not until Fort Norfolk was constructed during the War of 1812 did Turkey Point have anything like a permanent settlement and that, too, was abandoned at the close of the war. The crumbled remains of the earth and stake fort are still visible near the park's waterfront.

Camping is a good deal easier now than when the hearty Sulpicians bivouacked here but Turkey Point still retains a hint of wilderness. A medium-high bluff runs the length of the mile-long sand beach offering a raised lookout over Long Point Bay and the shallow blue-green waters of eastern Lake Erie.

Roughly twenty crow-flying miles apart are Selkirk and Rock Point recreation provincial parks. Selkirk, twenty-five miles northeast of Turkey Point, has a marshland similar to the western parks; as its name would suggest, Rock Point, to the east, offers a tougher geography.

About one-sixth of Selkirk is the wetland created by Sandusky Creek and a tributary stream where they enter Lake Erie. From here, the marsh covers the length of the park. It has the complete

Hank Babbitt

Lake Erie is a popular resort with boaters. Innumerable weather-worn piers (above) stretch far into the warm waters of every sandy bay. Beaches are the calling card for the Canadian parks that border Erie's north shore. Rondeau (right) is one of Ontario's oldest provincial parks.

range of bogside creatures from dragonflies to muskrats and the stream is a spawning bed for pike.

Rock Point features a small sand beach to the west side of its little peninsula. Around the tip and to the east, the shoreline is composed of shale rock, formed from sediments deposited by a Devonian sea 300 million years ago. Even the most unobservant hiker can find an abundance of fossilized sea life in the rocks. While Rock Point has no marshes as well defined as Selkirk's, it does have a few shallow pools where a variety of shorebirds feed.

At the mouth of the famous Niagara River (see Chapter 9), Ontario relinquishes Lake Erie to New York. However, only seventy miles of Erie edges

the state's northwest boundary. The New York State Thruway follows the coast, traversing the lakefront lowland which lifts inland toward the Appalachian foothills. What sectors of the lowland are not industrial are neat dairy and vegetable farms and vineyards.

Rimming this agricultural plain are the beaches of Evangola and Lake Erie state parks, just twenty-five miles apart, the only two state parks on the lake.

Ontario Ministry of Industry and Tourism

Picnickers, campers, fishermen and sunbathers migrate each summer to Evangola from Buffalo, thirty miles northeast, and to Lake Erie from Dunkirk, seven miles northeast. Both parks receive too much usage to have any wilderness appeal. Their hardwood trees are orderly and trim; shrubs and thickets have given way to playgrounds and ball fields.

Like these two city-ringed parks, Presque Isle State Park is the backyard for Erie, Pennsylvania.

Its narrow, hook-shaped peninsula forms the long breakwater for Erie's harbor on Presque Isle Bay.

Presque Isle has partially solved its population problem by turning away campers. The handsome park drive wends through a healthy hardwood forest, looping around the peninsula to face both Lake Erie to the north and quiet Presque Isle Bay to the south. Lake breezes sweep the beaches on the outer coast to cool the city-weary swimmers and sunbathers while bayside visitors have an

129

Joe Kirkish

The sun forces its way through the thick fog to shine on a docile lake. Reeds and beach grasses rim the shore.

excellent view of the foreign ships and Great Lakes freighters at work in Erie's harbor. Still ponds and lagoons lace the park's interior, speckling the forest with rest areas for migrating waterfowl.

At one time, Ohio's Lake Erie coast was almost all marshland. Most has been drained to accommodate several major cities and a ring of rich farmland. What bogs remain are now protected in various parks and wildlife refuges. Preserves like Headlands Beach State Park, about twenty-five miles northeast of downtown Cleveland, are almost entirely devoted to the plants and animals peculiar to wetlands. Headlands Beach is adjacent to Mentor Marsh where the rare prothonotary warbler nests. Hiking trails in the state park traverse the swamps.

Particularly extensive are the Lake Erie fens midway on the forty-mile coast between Toledo and Port Clinton. Three adjacent preserves restrict further encroachment on the life of the bogs.

Crane Creek Wildlife Experiment Station, better known as Magee Marsh, is second only to Point Pelee National Park in the varieties of birds that seek its protected reedy ponds. Waterfowl like Canada geese, mallards and blue-winged teal nest here, as do shorebirds such as bitterns and herons. Flocks of as many as five thousand whistling swans rustle and swoop through the marsh each March.

A park drive and foot trails rimming the bogs lead to the adjacent Crane Creek State Park. On the "bird trails" in the park and marsh, watchers can observe the waterfowl looking back from clumps of tall grasses and willowy sedges. The wetlands reach almost to Crane Creek's shore where its fine sandy beach is shaded by enormous cottonwoods. A new nature interpretive center and waterfowl museum describe the variety of life and the delicate balance of a swamp. To help maintain that balance, campers have been banned from Crane Creek.

Three national wildlife refuges protect the waterfowl that inhabit the Lake Erie domains of Ohio. Cedar Point resides on the tip of a marshy peninsula east of Toledo and West Sister Island is a tiny preserve in the Erie Islands. Ottawa National Wildlife Refuge, adjacent to Crane Creek State Park, is alive with nesting birds, 250 species in all. Even the reluctant bald eagle has been urged to build his high aerie far in the secluded backlands of the swamp.

The marshlands of Lake Erie have their own subtle beauty. Their very stillness, pierced solely by the sweet melody of a shy warbler or the grumpy honking of the geese, affords a special private world to those who walk the marsh trails.

131

Hank Babbitt

White pond lilies and yellow spatterdocks dance for the summer among the various greens of sedges, cattails and pickerel weeds. Then, in the fall, the fens blush pink as it is the marsh mallow's turn to blossom. A quiet world for a moment's solitude, a mecca for ornithologists — these are the lures of the Lake Erie marshes.

Equally delightful are the sites and parks of the Lake Erie islands. The little group is scattered about the waters north and east of Sandusky Bay.

The islands can be reached from Marblehead Peninsula which juts eastward into Lake Erie, forming the northern border of Sandusky Bay. Ferries from Port Clinton, Catawba Point and Sandusky daily chug to South Bass and Kelleys

islands. Also, the "Tin Goose," one of the last eleven Ford tri-motors still in flyable condition, carries mail, cargo and passengers to Put-in-Bay on South Bass Island.

On the Marblehead are two state parks. East Harbor features a two-and-one-half-mile sand beach, one of the best of Lake Erie. Catawba State Park, at the northern tip of the peninsula, is a tiny picnic site. Both parks have boat launch facilities for captains who prefer private tours of the islands to the auto-ferry rides.

Kelleys Island, the most easterly of the Lake Erie islands, is irrevocable evidence that enormous glaciers passed this way: especially at the north-west end of the island, where sharp trenches have

132

By extending its neck and beak upward, a least bittern (left) can escape detection by predators in its reedy, freshwater habitat. Lily pads (above), among the prettier tenants of Lake Erie's marshes, drift into a sun ray.

been carved six feet down through the island floor. These glacial grooves were whittled by rocks dragged along by a mile-thick glacier. The rocks were hard, sharp igneous boulders from Canada's Pre-Cambrian Shield; they readily scooped out the softer Devonian limestone of Kelleys Island. Ancient rock butchered ancient rock, leaving behind the deep glacial grooves which are now a state memorial. So, too, is Inscription Rock, on the southern tip of Kelleys Island, which is a limestone boulder carved with the mysterious pictographs of prehistoric peoples.

The neighbor to both the glacial grooves and Inscription Rock state memorials is Kelleys Island State Park. It, too, has the striations of glacial

movements as well as a small marsh. The hackberry and elm woods crowd up to the park's sandy beach.

South Bass Island, most populated and popular of the group, is a delightful conglomeration of natural and man-made sites. A rich maple and oak woods frosts the high limestone cliffs of South Bass Island State Park. Here in summer, overlooking little Stone's Cove near the south tip of the island, flotillas of sails bob in the aqua waters between the island and the mainland, three miles distant. The glacial grooves of South Bass are visible but not so deep as those of Kelleys.

The quaint village of Put-in-Bay resides on a narrow neck of land just northeast of the island's center. Here Commodore Perry's little squadron

H. Michael Brauer

The land beyond Lake Erie's northwestern shore, known as Ontario's Sun Parlor, is fertile farmland. The morning mist (above) shrouds the fields of a rustic farm. The boardwalk at Canada's Point Pelee National Park (right) yields an excellent view of life in the marshland. It is one of North America's finest locations to watch bird migrations.

rested the few days before the Battle of Lake Erie. Today, Put-in-Bay welcomes the squadrons of ferries and private yachts disgorging tourists to the island's beaches and fishermen to its bass-rich bays. Each August, the little resort town hosts the Inter-Lake Regatta, one of the country's largest sailboat racing competitions.

Commodore Perry and his battle are well-remembered in Put-in-Bay. It is the site of Perry's Cave, a deep limestone cavern where the commodore is said to have stored ammunition before the battle and British prisoners after. Within the cave, a deep still pool, the Wishing Well, ebbs and flows with the level of Lake Erie.

Also at Put-in-Bay is Perry's Victory and International Peace Memorial National Monument. The sleek, white granite Doric column pierces upward 352 feet, standing taller than the Statue of Liberty. It memorializes both the 1813 Battle of Lake Erie and peace through arbitration among nations. Within the monument is the Rush-Bagot Agreement of 1817, preserved in a bronze tablet. In a crypt beneath the monument are the remains of six officers, three American and three British, who died in the battle. An elevator rises to the observation platform atop the column which extends a stunning view of the surrounding islands, blue waters and mainlands of both Canada and the

Ontario Ministry of Industry and Tourism

United States. At night, the monument is floodlit and lifts in stark and haughty grandeur to crown the Lake Erie islands.

Crystal Cave is perhaps South Bass Island's most unique formation. A brilliant cluster of crystals cover every inch of the cave's ceiling and walls. The prismatic shards drip to lengths of eighteen inches, reflecting a dazzling spectrum of colors. No place else in the United States rivals this extensive deposit of strontium sulphate crystals.

Michigan is the last state to rejoin Lake Erie with the Detroit River and Ontario. This twenty-five mile strip of land, between the river and Toledo, is largely an industrial corridor. Sterling State Park, near Monroe, is the only major public preserve. Its sparse, airy woods shelter the picnic and campgrounds inland from the long sandy beach. Lake Erie is quite shallow here at its western end so Sterling is a safe swimming beach.

Erie is a troubled lake, known for its pollution problems, its violent temper and its industrial complexes. But it is also known for its lovely freshwater marshes, sandy beaches and delightful islands. As men worked to destroy it, they now work to save it. What is bad is being corrected; what is good is here now, luring waterfowl to the marshes and people to the shores.

135

ONTARIO
The Beautiful Lake

Ancestors of the Iroquois looked over the sparkling blue-green expanse, settled near its sloping banks and named the lake Ontario, the Beautiful Lake. Its charms spoke to the white men, too; as many as three centuries ago, Champlain and Brulé, the Jesuits and LaSalle all paddled along the beautiful lake's sandy shores. Like Huron, Lake Ontario is deeply immersed in Canadian history.

The littlest Great Lake of all, Ontario is a kinder lake than Erie. While smaller by about 2,500 square miles, its greater depths are not so easily churned by a passing wind; Ontario's storms are ferocious but they give greater warning of their approach. Its depth also causes it to remain cool long into the spring and warm to the brink of winter, tempering the flat lands around it to bear rich harvests in vast fruit orchards. New York to the south and Ontario to the north are the lake's only neighbors; Canada claims the major share of the 7,300 square miles.

Waters from all the other Great Lakes tumble into Ontario through the Niagara River, then push eastward at a surface current of about eight miles per hour, flow through the Thousand Islands of the St. Lawrence and follow the river through the seaway to the sea.

The mighty river, the Niagara, which connects Lake Ontario to the rest also divided it from early Great Lakes shipping. The tons of water barreling over the enormous Niagara Falls, causing wild currents to plunge through the deep-torn gorge below the falls, made the river impassable. Ships sailing Lake Ontario could not cross the barrier to gather Chicago goods; ships built in Cleveland could not navigate the river en route to the sea. Not until 1829, when the Welland Canal was built to the west of the river, connecting lakes Erie and Ontario, did Lake Ontario truly join the Great Lakes chain.

The Niagara, a section of the Canada-United States border, is only about thirty-five rugged miles long. It runs approximately south to north, dropping some 326 feet from Lake Erie into lower Lake Ontario. The river traverses the tough limestone of the Niagara Escarpment where it has laboriously been digging its bed deep into the rock until it now flows through a narrow, magnificent gorge.

Since the falls were first spotted by Father Hennepin in the late seventeenth century, the beauties of the river have been extolled by both Canadians and Americans; by the mid-1800's, its falls were already a favorite tourist attraction. Hawkers barked their wares along its steep banks, sideshows exhibited their freaks, flim-flam men gulled tourists for whatever they could get. The honky-tonk atmosphere, the swindlers and thieves so infested "the Front" that the Niagara became as infamous as it was famous. Soon the chagrined officials of both Ontario and New York stepped in to supervise the tourist center. So it was that, as early as the 1880's, stretches of the Niagara came under government protection. Consequently, the

In midwinter, the spray from Niagara Falls freezes, encasing the surrounding trees, rocks and guard rails in ice sheaths. In the background is the Canadian cascade, Horseshoe Falls.

river is still a lovely mecca for boaters and campers and the falls, of course, for honeymooners.

New York has sprinkled the Niagara with state parks. At the river's southern end, it is wide and lazy; it has not yet mustered the reckless speed it will gain as it thrashes downward toward the falls. The river splits into West and East branches to circle Grand Island, a river wayside that is bigger than Manhattan. Circling the island along with the river is a flotilla of grand private yachts and sleek sailboats, for the Niagara is a boater's delight. Similarly, its perch fishing draws the smaller boats.

To service the boaters, Grand Island has two state parks, which can also be reached from the mainland via the scenic parkways that ring the island. Beaver Island State Park, at the southern tip of Grand Island, has a fine boat harbor near its wide, sandy beach. This is a developed area as the beach is backed by a boardwalk, cafe and golf course. The wild things are reserved for Buckhorn Island State Park at the northern end of Grand. It will never be developed into a "country club" sort of park; instead, its marshy flats and reedy meadows are a sanctuary for waterfowl and lower bog life. Only a short nature trail interrupts the serenity.

The parkways of Grand Island connect with the Robert Moses State Parkway which parallels the river on the New York side until it arrives at Lake Ontario. It begins midway down the river, near the falls and the Niagara Reservation.

This reservation, run by the Niagara Frontier State Park Commission, encompasses the mainland as well as Goat Island, which splits the falls into two cascades, American Falls and Horseshoe Falls (the latter owned by Ontario). Near the rim of the gorge, the new Schoellkopf Geological Museum features exhibits on the geology and history of Niagara Falls.

The American Falls, 1,075 feet at the brink, tumbles 182 feet into the gorge below; the semi-circular, 2,100-foot-wide Horseshoe Falls descends 176 feet. More water crashes over the Horseshoe than the American, making it an ever-changing kaleidoscope of sparkling emerald hues. About 41.4 million gallons plunge over the Horseshoe every minute, while 3.6 million gallons per minute navigate the American Falls. The gorge that Niagara Falls has drilled into the limestone at its base is 350 feet deep and the churning water rises to 190 feet within it before escaping on its way downriver.

Niagara Falls can be seen from every conceivable vantage point. Elevators at the observation tower in Niagara Reservation soar above them for a

breathtaking panorama and plunge underground to the gorge at the American Falls' base. Similarly, elevators tunnel into the gorge from Table Rock House on the Canadian side for a close-up look in front or in back of the Horseshoe Falls (waterproof slickers are provided). Helicopters fly over the falls; boat tours cross the tumultuous gorge below. A middle view, especially appealing at night when color lights illuminate the falls, is provided from Rainbow Bridge just downriver from the cascade. From Goat Island (and tiny Luna and Three Sister islands) viewpoints overlook the brink of the water just as it spills away.

Goat Island is a pretty little woodland reached from the mainland by both foot and auto bridges. From it, too, elevators chisel downward to the gorge where the wild waters, so very few feet away, howl out in fearsome thunder. From the trail along the gorge the sprays of Bridal Veil Fall, a watery splinter separated from the American Falls by tiny Luna Island, enfold the hiker in a misty shroud.

All of the water that crashes over the falls is funneled into the steep and slender gorge. Caught in such narrow confines, the angry river strains to be free; ferocious rapids and Herculean currents battle the rock-ribbed cradle until the river is released to the quiet calm of Lake Ontario.

To the east of the gorge, the twenty-mile-long picturesque Robert Moses Parkway skirts the industrial city of Niagara Falls and, further north, the rich, colorful orchards of Niagara country. To the west, the parkway gives access to a handful of small state parks devoted to the scenery of the gorge. Each of these lower Niagara parks is prettily forested with hardwoods that color in the fall and each is crossed with narrow nature paths that wind downward into the gorge to the riverside.

Whirlpool State Park, just three miles north of the falls, overlooks a violent maelstrom cut three hundred feet into the earth by endless years of scouring water. The river plunges into the whirlpool through its narrow chasm and churns around in a complete circle before escaping once more on its way to Lake Ontario. The thunder here is almost as deafening as that of the mighty falls itself.

Also perched atop the three-hundred-foot ravine is Devils Hole State Park. Steps and trails teeter down to the river's edge, while the spectacular view from above overlooks the last of the Niagara rapids and the first section of navigable river. At Devils Hole, in the fall of 1763, a marauding band of Senecas, angered by the loss of the French fur trade, forced two British wagon trains over the brink of the gorge, catapulting them into the wild

*Two costumed guards protect Old Fort Niagara at the
Gate of the Five Nations, which is operated by a system of
chains, windlasses and counterbalance weights of stone.*

river below. Downriver from Devils Hole, three more state parks — Lewiston, Lower Niagara River and Joseph Davis — overlook the calmer waters and traffic of the widening Niagara as it moves toward the lake.

At the junction of the river and Lake Ontario, surrounded by the wooded landscape and white sandy beach of Fort Niagara State Park, is the splendid restoration of Old Fort Niagara. The sturdy old citadel was built so well in 1726 that it still stands two and one-half centuries later.

The original structure looks less like a fort than a French castle. The French called it a trading post and secluded its mighty fortifications beneath its decorative design to fool the ever-wary Iroquois. Today the castle has been furnished in the period of Louis XV; also restored are the military kitchen, dungeon, Jesuit chapel and the medieval-style drawbridge at the Gate of the Five Nations (apparently so named in an attempt to pander to the Iroquois). This fort entrance operates by chains, windlasses and counter-balance weights of stone. Through the years and wars of New France, the British and colonists each had possession of Old Fort Niagara; the buildings and structures added during their tenancy have also been restored. Today, the period flags of all three nations fly over the noble old fortress which still stands guard over the Niagara with its fifty-three antique cannons.

Just two miles east of the fort is a new addition to Fort Niagara State Park called the Four Mile Creek Annex. With a beach on Lake Ontario, the shady annex is the campground from which all the Niagara sites can be visited.

While New York has many fine parks on the river, the land between them is not under government control. Consequently, parts of the riverside are heavily commercial and the natural appeal is lost. The Ontario government showed a bit more forethought when, before the turn of the century, it deeded the entire riverfront to the Niagara Parks Commission. Therefore, the thirty-five-mile river, rimmed on the Ontario side by the Niagara Scenic Parkway, is a continuous chain of protected lands and tourist attractions.

Old Fort Erie, as it stands today on the southern end of the Niagara Scenic Parkway, is the third citadel on the site. The first, built by the British in 1764, and the second were both buffeted and damaged by the querulous weather of Lake Erie; the third fort was more prudently located a bit upriver, away from the lakeshore. The barracks buildings of the fort contain a fine collection of weapons and relics found during restoration.

(continued on page 143)

Niagara Frontier State Park Commission

Old Fort Niagara dominates the junction of Lake Ontario and the Niagara River. The sturdy fortress is two and a half centuries old, built by the French to keep an eye on the Iroquois.

While numerous on the East Coast, the ringbilled gull is less common to the Great Lakes than the herring gull. The dark band around its beak gives the ringbilled its name.

A sense of history is alive all along the Niagara Scenic Parkway. At the one end is Fort Erie, at the other, Fort George. Built of squared logs just before the War of 1812, the fort was destroyed by the Americans. Its buildings have been restored and, like Fort Erie, it is now manned by guards dressed in period uniforms. Not far outside its twelve-foot-high stockade is old Navy Hall. In 1792, the first parliament of Upper Canada was held here and today the historic hall is a museum of bygone wars and pioneer days.

Between them on the parkway, the citadels overlook several other historic landmarks. On the riverside, viewing the upper river rapids and Navy Island, a Canadian game preserve, is marvelous old Oak Hall. Five of the thirty-seven rooms in the nineteenth-century limestone mansion have been decorated with furnishings from the original home. Downriver, where the Niagara broadens toward Lake Ontario, is the Georgian-style McFarland House. Its style, dating back to 1800, is indicative of the days when settlers, disgusted with their damp and drafty log cabins, were remodeling homes with stout, handmade bricks. The house was used as a hospital in the War of 1812 by both the British and Americans (like a ping-pong ball, the Niagara kept changing sides throughout the match) and today is refurbished in period furnishings.

Neighboring the McFarland House are the grounds of Queenston Heights. This famous battlefield of the War of 1812 is now a handsome park. Reigning over it and the sloping banks of the lower Niagara is the 210-foot-high stone memorial to General Isaac Brock, a British hero of the war.

Downriver from Fort Erie, overlooking Grand Island, is little Miller's Creek Park. Canadians use the boat launch here to mingle their vessels with the American traffic on the slow-moving upper Niagara. This is one of only two campgrounds easily accessible from the parkway; the other, Charles Daley Park, is west of the Niagara on Lake Ontario. Daley Park was farmland in the 1800's so fruit orchards, now growing wild, shade its airy meadows. A beach has been built on the lake for the little park which is located between Fifteen- and Sixteen-Mile Creeks, named by early settlers to mark their approximate mileage west from the Niagara River.

As previously mentioned, Ontario, like New York, has its own elevators and observation lookouts at Niagara Falls. In fact, the view of the falls is generally superior on the Canadian side; the huge Horseshoe Falls seen in profile tumbles in countless shades of green, sprinkling visitors with a fine, icy spray. Often a rainbow arcs through the mist like a canopy over the deep, swirling gorge far below.

The most appealing site of the Niagara Scenic Parkway is the wildest. Lush Niagara Glen is aglimmer with trilliums and wild ginger nestled beneath tulip trees, sassafras, and red mulberry, a rare stranger to the Canadian forest. This virginal wilderness climbs the cliffs of the Niagara gorge opposite New York's Whirlpool State Park. It is a lesson in geology as the cliffs clearly show where the river has cut through three levels of time.

The upper layer is a fifty-foot-thick level of the Niagara Escarpment, cut through by the river eight thousand years ago. Coral sediments dropped by warm seas three hundred million years ago were molded into dull gray dolomite. Separated from this top layer by crumbly black shale is another limestone belt. The lowest layer is a band of white sandstone and red shale. Through all this the Niagara has sliced to its present bed.

Lovely trails traverse the woodland and cliffs of the Niagara Glen. The leaf-coated walkways, secluded and steep, wedge between huge fallen boulders (one such pass is called Fat Man's Misery), circle smooth potholes and trees which cling with clawlike roots to the tough, rock walls, and descend to the pebbly shores of the fast-running river. Most people come to the Niagara to see the falls; once they have done that, they come to see the Glen.

The wild, but still fruit-bearing, orchards of Charles Daley Park reveal the fertile lands of the Niagara Peninsula. This forty-mile-long Canadian land bridge separates the waters of lakes Erie and Ontario. At its northeast end, at the mouth of the river, is quaint, tree-lined Niagara-on-the-Lake; at its northwest end, also the westernmost point on Lake Ontario, is Hamilton, Ontario's steel capital.

The peninsula is primarily formed by the Niagara Escarpment but just to the north of the limestone belt is a wide fertile plain. Here is a mild farmland, rich in cherries, grapes and even peaches. The delightful inroads through the bright orchards create a cheery backdrop for Lake Ontario's southwestern shore. In May, the fruit trees blossom; in September, the grapes are picked to produce fifteen million gallons of wine. In the midst of the pastoral fields of the Niagara Peninsula it is possible to see ocean ships and lake freighters because the land is sliced through its center by the Welland Canal. The twenty-seven-mile stairway of ship locks descends from Port Colborne on Lake Erie to the Lake Ontario terminus, Port Weller in the city of St. Catharines.

Glaciers and now erosion have scraped layers of soft sediment away from harder sandstone to give Chimney Bluffs State Park in New York its unique conical formations.

Beneath it, the old Welland River runs through six huge concrete pipes.

Unlike Erie, Lake Ontario has many cities clustered about its northern shore. Between Hamilton on the west and Kingston on the east are Mississauga, Toronto, Oshawa and Cobourg. Trenton and Belleville border the narrow Bay of Quinte. The Canadian land that borders the lake, called the Golden Horseshoe, houses half the population of Ontario. Some day it will be one enormous lakefront megalopolis; today, the thirty-mile-long coast between Hamilton and Toronto almost is.

Among the offices and industries, however, touches of wilderness deny the encroachment of city lights. Provincial parks such as Darlington interrupt the monotony of traffic jams and urban renewal. This recreation provincial park is the hot summer beach, the brilliant autumn forest and the giant fishing hole just outside the automotive manufacturer, Oshawa. A similar oasis on the urbanized shore is Presqu'ile Provincial Park. The large natural environment reserve drops down on its own hook-shaped peninsula south of the apple orchards around Brighton. Presqu'ile is one of the few Lake Ontario parks large enough to have hiking trails through a handsome hardwood landscape. Across the quiet inlet formed by its peninsula, Presqu'ile overlooks Prince Edward country.

This large piece of land jutting into the lake is fundamentally a ragged-shored sandbar that emerged across the mouth of a great prehistoric bay whose modern day remains are the Bay of Quinte. From this ignoble beginning as a quicksilver sand lump, Prince Edward Peninsula has grown into a bustling summer resort.

Due to the indiscretion of early fortune hunters, the pleasures of Prince Edward were almost lost. The peninsula was mowed down by lumber barons. Consequently, the shallow top soil, laboriously deposited over long centuries, eroded away when the ground cover was depleted; as one huge gritty mound, the unleashed sands of Prince Edward began to shift. Drifting unchecked, this sugary-white mountain engulfed businesses and homes, smothering a church, hotel and various farms.

H. Armstrong Roberts

Man's reclamation of Prince Edward has been nearly as laborious as nature's task of building it in the first place. Ground cover, even the lowliest forms, found no pleasure in the free-drifting sands and sought no refuge there. So hay and straw mulches were added to the sands, sheltered by an extensive system of wind barriers. Slowly the hesitant shrubs and grasses returned; manually planted trees were coaxed to take root. When the reluctant forest finally caught on, it bloomed into a charming woodland that is stabilizing the shifting sand and taming the dunes. Prince Edward is a living example of man's ability to rebuild some of the beauty he has recklessly destroyed.

The peninsula is nearly an island; on the map it resembles a Rorschach inkblot. Its body joins the mainland only at a narrow land neck at its western end called the Carrying Place (once an Indian portage between Lake Ontario and the Bay of Quinte). Tiny inlets between outstretched land fingers are ringed with picturesque marinas, nine-teenth-century structures, antique shops and lake-side resorts. Sailing relics lure visitors to the Mariners Lighthouse Museum near Milford as do the pioneer artifacts of the Early Settler's Museum at Waupoos. Scenic backroads meander to the ancient lighthouse at Point Petre, the peninsula's southernmost tip, and continue to high lookouts amid the dunes that survey the Bay of Quinte, Lake Ontario, inland forests, hummocks and hills.

The high vantage points also overlook the miles of parks rimming Prince Edward's shores. North Beach Provincial Park, twelve miles south of Trenton, is one of Ontario's oldest, deeded to the government in 1835. The sunny resort is on a sandbar of its own between Lake Ontario and Lake North Bay. Beaches on both accommodate summer crowds although the inland lake's shore is shorter and steeper. Here, too, on brisk April evenings, anglers armed with nets, buckets and hip boots

Tons of Great Lakes water plunge over the American Falls at Niagara Falls on its way to Lake Ontario. In the background is Horseshoe Falls, separated from the American Falls by Goat Island.

greet the annual smelt run. From an island ten miles offshore, the blinking eye of Scotch Bonnet Lighthouse watches the activities of the busy park.

More magnificent than the sand flats of North Beach are the massive dunes of Sandbanks Provincial Park which slope steeply into the Great Lake, making the beach dangerous for inexperienced swimmers. This natural environment park, twenty-five miles south of Belleville, is the largest and wildest on Prince Edward; the only interlopers into its interior are hardy climbers who tackle its shimmering rows of dunes. Most walkers are content to negotiate the park's five-mile shore. Efforts for land reclamation at Sandbanks have been particularly diligent and difficult; still, the slipping and drifting of the enormous mounds is under precarious control.

The scenic egress from Prince Edward country is via the little ferry that chugs from Glenora back to the "mainland." From here, the shoreline drive travels the thirty-mile coast to Kingston. For three hundred years, since Frontenac founded it in 1673, the delightful and stately city has viewed the waters of Lake Ontario where they tumble into the St. Lawrence River. High on a bluff overlooking the strategic location and the old homes, schools and cathedrals of Kingston, stalwart Old Fort Henry still stands guard.

Begun in 1812, the mammoth fortress was redesigned in the 1830's. Old Fort Henry never saw a battle nor fired an angry shot but was, nevertheless, an active garrison until 1891. Today, within the thick embrasured walls of the near-perfect restoration, a living past is found. Old Fort Henry is immense with 126 rooms furnished as they were when British troops brandished weapons of war. Commanders still bark their orders and the rumble of cannon still resounds when the scarlet-uniformed Fort Henry Guard presents precision drills, artillery salutes with ancient muzzle-loaders and parades of fife-and-drum bands. In tiny artisan shops, craftsmen shape the same utilitarian wares their ancestors created over a century ago.

Across the wide, island-choked mouth of the St. Lawrence, New York reaches out to reclaim Lake Ontario's waters. Here, on a little peninsula that curls around Chaumont Bay near the river mouth, tiny Long Point State Park offers its sandy beach to sunny days while platoons of ocean-worthy long ships silently pass to and from the river, mighty corridor between lakes and sea.

New York, between the Niagara and St. Lawrence, improvidently allowed most of Lake Ontario's scenic shore to slip away. But it is reclaiming what it can; eleven preserves have been established along the coast. Many of these state parks, like Wescott Beach on Henderson Bay and Southwick Beach near the town of Woodville, are well developed. Their most popular features are their wide, sandy beaches.

Lake Ontario's historic sites are as guarded by New York as they are by Ontario. Sackets Harbor Battlefield, near the resort village of the same name, is a memorial to the conflict fought here in the War of 1812. Its military cemetery is the burial place of General Zebulon Pike, discoverer of Pikes Peak in Colorado.

On the right bank of the Oswego River, overlooking its entry to Lake Ontario, Fort Ontario stands quiet and austere. But its steep scarp walls have known the clamorous strife of the French and Indian War, the American Revolution and the War of 1812. Built originally by the British to pester the French traders in 1755, Fort Ontario occupies one of the oldest fortified sites on the Great Lakes. It has been destroyed twice, first by the French in 1756, then the British in 1812; that it was always rebuilt gives credence to the strategic import of its location.

Today's Fort Ontario is the nineteenth-century version. Not as elaborate as Old Fort Henry, it still has appealing reconstructions of the powder magazine, barracks, guard house and officers' quarters. Each is furnished in period decor.

Fort Ontario is nearly the midpoint on the thirty-mile coastline between two state parks. Selkirk Shores, to the east, is one thousand acres of hiking trails, play fields and airy, landscaped woods. The waves that greet its lengthy beach are gentled by two long jetties used by youngsters to challenge the lake perch. To the west of the fort, Fair Haven Beach State Park is nearly as large as Selkirk Shores. Lofty bluffs near the park's eastern boundary soar above Lake Ontario, reaching the highest elevation found anywhere on the lake's normally flat shore. Sweeping away from the bluffs, Fair Haven Beach stretches to its end at a picturesque Federal lighthouse and pier.

One of the most intriguing lakeshore parks is not yet developed for public use. Tall, spirelike rock shafts have given Chimney Bluffs State Park its name. Along with Fair Haven Beach, Chimney Bluffs is the northern border of central New York's Finger Lakes region and, consequently, shares some of its unique geography.

Soft shales and slates, first scarred and lacerated by glacial bulldozing and now badgered by erosion,

(continued on page 151)

Travelpic Publications

The St. Lawrence River strains the water of Lake Ontario through a sieve of islands; a cruise boat navigates the narrow channels between the Thousand Islands.

On a sunny summer day at any sandy beach, visitors can make the most of the cool, foamy surf. This scene is repeated across the Great Lakes wherever rock cliffs give way to sugary sand.

*A common tern lands amid beach grass. Its small
feet make it a weak swimmer, but it is a tireless flyer that
swoops down to the water, seizing prey as it wings by.*

were eaten away from tougher strata of sandstone. What remains at Chimney Bluffs are jagged cliffs and irregular formations jutting through a hemlock, cedar and pine forest.

West of Rochester, the lakeshore once more gives way to flatter lands. Three more state parks are linked by the Lake Ontario State Parkway, a thirty-mile scenic drive which, rimmed with clumps of flowering crabapple, moves along the coast.

Lakeside Beach State Park, western terminus of the parkway, is the smallest of the three and its grounds are given over primarily to campers. Braddock Bay State Park, the largest and closest to Rochester, is nearly as much water as land. The park is riddled with reedy ponds and for every pond there is a creek, for every creek a small marshland. Around this spongy interior is a superior beach with a host of visitor facilities. Between these two parkway preserves is busy Hamlin Beach State Park with its three sunny beaches that attract enormous crowds.

As the New York coast dips southwest toward the mouth of the Niagara, its shoreline becomes even more congested. Golden Hill and Wilson-Tuscarora state parks, twenty and thirty miles east of the river, must handle a bulk of the traffic en route to the falls. Both parks work year-round, featuring spring fishing, summer camp-outs, picnics and beach parties, colorful autumn hardwood stands and winter sports facilities. Wilson-Tuscarora is in the final stages of development and the campground at Golden Hill is newly completed.

Lake Ontario is the clearinghouse for the Great Lakes. Waters that have licked Chicago or frozen in Thunder Bay pour into Lake Ontario via the Niagara to mingle at last for their final rest. Then, caught by the incessant tugging of the St. Lawrence, the Great Lakes ripple and swirl outward to be lost in the sea.

ST. LAWRENCE RIVER

The Vital Link

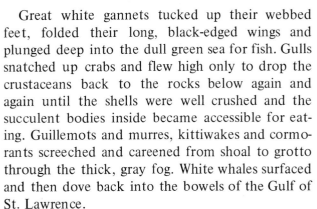

Great white gannets tucked up their webbed feet, folded their long, black-edged wings and plunged deep into the dull green sea for fish. Gulls snatched up crabs and flew high only to drop the crustaceans back to the rocks below again and again until the shells were well crushed and the succulent bodies inside became accessible for eating. Guillemots and murres, kittiwakes and cormorants screeched and careened from shoal to grotto through the thick, gray fog. White whales surfaced and then dove back into the bowels of the Gulf of St. Lawrence.

These were the greeters that met Jacques Cartier in 1535, when he maneuvered three frail vessels through the long gulf to become the first white man to sail the St. Lawrence River. For six hundred miles Cartier followed the river in search of China, down to the island of present-day Montreal. Here his three ships were stopped by foaming, tumbling rapids; in bitter irony, Cartier named them Lachine, the Chinese rapids. After a devastating winter, Cartier returned to France, his dreams of a passage to the Orient still unfulfilled.

Others would follow Cartier in the decades to come, tracing the St. Lawrence inland. Canada is the child of this river; through it, the country was discovered, the riches of the interior were extracted, warring armies battled for possession. The provinces of Ontario and Quebec share its rocky

Quebec City's Citadel, a fortress of twenty-five buildings built in the early 1800's, looks across the St. Lawrence from its high perch on Cape Diamond to Ile d'Orléans and Cape Tourmente.

Travelpic Publications

153

The Thousand Islands Bridge spans the upper St. Lawrence River, resting on two Canadian national park islands between Ontario and New York. The panorama of the islands from the bridge is superb.

northern banks; to the south, New York claims one hundred miles before relinquishing the remaining 650 miles to Quebec.

Of all North American rivers, the St. Lawrence is one of the most beautiful. From Kingston, Ontario, at its mouth on Lake Ontario, to Montreal, it sang with the musical thunder of rapids; it was this gorgeous white water that impeded all traffic, even the canoes of the most skillful Iroquois, on the upper river. Today, the St. Lawrence Seaway has flooded some rapids and by-passed others to welcome ocean vessels onto the Great Lakes. Downriver from Montreal, and onward toward the Atlantic, the river is deep and slow. Where the Saguenay River enters it, 125 miles north of Quebec City, the depth of the St. Lawrence is 880 feet; at its entrance into the ocean it yawns to a ninety-mile width. The lower St. Lawrence is framed to the north by the Laurentian Mountains and to the south by the Chic-Chocs. Ocean freighters easily cruise its deep, straight channel, unhindered by rapids or falls.

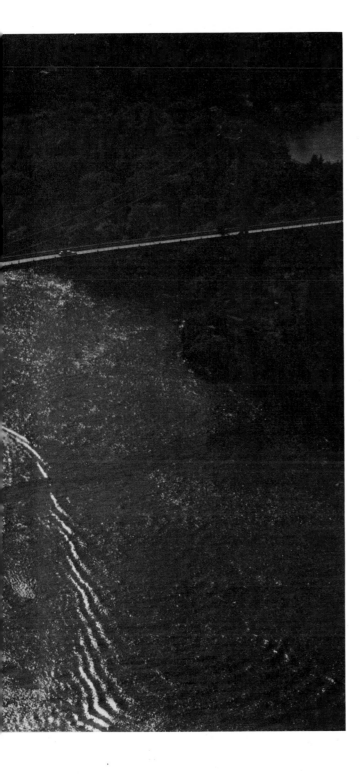

All together, the islands total about one thousand acres, making St. Lawrence Islands the smallest national park in Canada. Yet it is alive with its own charms, unequalled in many larger preserves. Centuries ago the Iroquois who camped on these islands honored their beauty by calling them *Manitoana*, Garden of the Great Spirit.

Before the Ice Age forced a drainage canal, predecessor to the St. Lawrence, from the Great Lakes to the sea, the Thousand Islands were hilltops and the river channels their valleys. They are outcroppings of the same branch of the Canadian Shield that ends up as New York's Adirondack Mountains. Their solid bedrock is the granite, gneiss and quartzite of Pre-Cambrian days. So they stand immovable and strong, their rugged boulders piercing the moist forest floor.

Enormous old oaks and hickories mingle with more airy maples and butternuts; these are all trees of the deciduous forest of North America. Since the islands are on the northeast limits of this forest, much of their vegetation is more common in Southern regions. The ebony spleenwort fern seeks the shade of such shrubs as witch hazel, arrowwood and redroots, which, in turn, nestle against red juniper and pitch pine, both rare visitors to the Canadian forest. This original vegetation is best seen in the pristine areas of Georgina and Mulcaster islands; many of the others have suffered past lumbering and burns.

The islands are too small for large animals with the exception of white-tailed deer. Cottontails and raccoons rule the ground while, above them, song sparrows nest. Screaming clouds of ring-billed gulls circle the short coastlines and spotted sandpipers patrol the shores.

Mingling with St. Lawrence Islands National Park are the half-dozen island state parks of New York. From the Lake Ontario river mouth, they run down river to Morristown, New York, across the St. Lawrence from Brockville, while on the mainland are a half-dozen more. Their forests and grounds are similar to those of the national park although not quite so untouched; all offer picnic sites and boat ramps, beaches and ball fields. Hugh Wellesley Island State Park, 2,610 acres, even has a golf course. Fishermen come to these islands to camp by night and seek the river's muskellunge, black bass and pike by day. Similarly, the parks are excellent starting points for glorious sailing amidst the Thousand Islands.

The north shore mainland of the upper St. Lawrence is nearly as entertaining as the islands. It is traversed by the Thousand Islands Parkway, one

The upper St. Lawrence, from Kingston to Brockville, fifty miles away, is studded with an emerald green wonderland. Here the Thousand Islands (actually numbering closer to 1,800) stuff the river mouth with cool, forested oases ringed with tiny pinpoints of Pre-Cambrian rock supporting solitary pitch pines. Between them, the international border of Canada and the United States snakes and winds, following the erratic path of the river channels. Seventeen of the major islands and eighty rocky islets have been set aside for Canada's St. Lawrence Islands National Park.

long corridor of riverfront parks where camp-grounds and boat ramps feed even more visitors to the islands. Resort cities like Gananoque offer boat tours of the islands; Ivy Lea is the terminus for the Thousand Islands Bridge which rests on three islands, two of them in the national park, en route from New York to Ontario. On one, Hill Island, a modern tower called the Skydeck soars to four hundred feet for an exciting panorama of the river, islands, MacIntosh apple orchards far to the north and the mainlands of two countries.

East of Brockville, one of Ontario's most charming little cities where tree-lined streets are dominated by dignified old mansions and fountains, the islands begin to yield to a clear, open stretch of river. Fifteen miles downriver, at Prescott, Ontario, and, across the river, Ogdensburg, New York, the St. Lawrence Seaway begins.

This enormous system of locks, dams and canals was perhaps the biggest project ever undertaken by two governments. The old canal system that predated the seaway was too shallow and narrow to allow large ocean vessels access to the Great Lakes. For decades the river was studied to develop a superior route. Canada and the United States began work on the new seaway in 1954; in 1959, it was complete. Between the two dates, an artificial lake was built as were two powerhouses, two dams and seven new locks.

From the Lake Ontario entrance to its mouth, the St. Lawrence drops 225 feet. Most of this drop formerly was in three sets of rapids above Montreal: the Long Sault, the Soulange and the Lachine.

The Long Sault Rapids, east of the Thousand Islands, dropped ninety treacherous feet, buffeting tons of white water over a bed of pre-glacial boulders. This entire area was flooded to produce a calm, deep lake that ships could pass over and that would become a huge power pool. To create this pool, the Iroquois Dam was built near Prescott and a powerhouse (jointly owned by the two countries and crossing the international border) was constructed over the 3,300 feet from Barnhart Island to Cornwall, Ontario, fifty miles downriver from Prescott. Finally, a giant spillway to control the depth of the power pool was erected upriver from the powerhouse.

The power pool that now rests easily where the Long Sault once raged is called Lake St. Lawrence. In reality it is a wide spot on the river, over thirty miles long and one to four miles wide. This is one of the largest artificial lakes ever built. To create it, three towns and four villages plus hundreds of farms were destroyed; according to the occupants' wishes, old homes were moved or new homes built

Quebec Tourist Branch

156

*The St. Lambert Lock at Montreal helps lift a ship over
the same rapids that stymied Cartier in 1535. In the background are
lights from the international exhibitions of Man and His World.*

Quebec Tourist Branch

Tadoussac, Quebec (above), where the Saguenay River meets the St. Lawrence, is the site of the first French home in Canada, built in 1599. Seen from the Plains of Abraham at Quebec City, an ocean freighter (right) cruises the majestic river.

along the banks of the new lake. New townsites were constructed to replace the old, now buried beneath the St. Lawrence.

One lock at the Iroquois Dam lowers an eastbound ship six feet onto Lake St. Lawrence. After traversing the quiet lake to its eastern end, south of the spillway and powerhouse, the ship enters a ten-mile canal through two more locks, the Eisenhower and the Snell, to be lowered ninety more feet. Immediately, the eastbound ship sails beneath the International Bridge, a high-level suspension span from Cornwall, Ontario, to Rooseveltown, New York, and travels another thirty tranquil miles to the next set of twin locks that drop eighty-two feet around the Soulange Rapids. The final section of the new St. Lawrence Seaway is at Montreal where two locks, the Côte Ste. Catherine and the St. Lambert, lower the ship the final fifty-two feet around the same Lachine Rapids that baffled Cartier back in 1535. Just 424 years later, man had opened the interior to the sea; the wealth of the Great Lakes could mingle with the wealth of the

world. From Montreal to the Atlantic, the St. Lawrence is a naturally wide, deep shipping canal.

Near each new lock, observation platforms allow close-up views of the seaway at work. From the Ontario towns of the north shore, Prescott, Morrisburg and Cornwall, views of ocean liners are as common as canoes once were.

Besides its grandstand seat at the west end of the seaway, Prescott enjoys another impressive sight. The lofty palisades of Fort Wellington National Park rise to the east, above the little industrial

159

town. The fort, built in the War of 1812, made Prescott the main base of defense for communications between Montreal and Kingston. Within its walls, the officers' quarters are decorated in late-Sheraton or Regency style and the massive blockhouse, three stories of stone, is a museum of fort artifacts.

Just as the St. Lawrence was the route into the Canadian heartland for explorers, so, too, did the earliest settlers follow the muscular waterway. The villages of the St. Lawrence are ancient; many still harbor eighteenth- and nineteenth-century structures. Consequently, when the Long Sault was to be flooded to form Lake St. Lawrence, many historic old buildings were endangered. In an enlightened burst of forethought, the Ontario government saved them. From villages scattered over the thousands of acres destined for inundation, dozens of aged structures were painstakingly moved to safe ground. Today they are gathered together on the riverbank in Upper Canada Village, fifteen miles from Cornwall, the most easterly city in Ontario.

Every detail, from door latches to pegs, is authentic in this charming village, making it a complete representation of an early nineteenth-century Canadian settlement. Time is rolled back to an era of hand tools, butter churns and long gowns; costumed artisans spin and weave, make blankets in the woolen mill, serve Old-World delights in the Willard Hotel. A farm, church, schoolmaster's house, doctor's office and general store are completely restored; from the little bake shop, sweet odors of freshly baked goods waft over the village. The serenity of Upper Canada Village is complete, jostled only when the lumber mill whines or an oxcart or stage coach rumbles by.

Giving the village a velvety green border are the manicured grounds of Crysler's Farm Battlefield Park, a tribute to the gallant troops who fought here in the War of 1812. The Memorial Mound rises near the river and the grassy mall leading to it is flanked by British oaks and Canadian maples.

The St. Lawrence offers no finer site than Canada's largest city, Montreal. At this island in the heart of the river, where the Ottawa empties into it, Cartier came to an Indian village named Hochelaga. Fifty long, bark-covered homes were surrounded by a triple palisade. Above Hochelaga, forested Mount Royal rose to 750 feet.

The beautiful island is now a beautiful city. Modern skyscrapers mingle with eighteenth- and nineteenth-century churches and homes. The city's island is thirty miles long, nine miles wide and houses 2.5 million residents, about sixty-five per-

cent of them French-speaking. Two smaller neighboring islands host the ever-changing Man and His World, a collage of exhibits displaying international cultures and industries that was built for the 1967 world's fair, Expo '67. Rising above this cosmopolitan city, the peak of Mount Royal is a wooded parkland where horse-drawn carriages clop along beside pools and lakes where waterfowl bicker and quack. From this summit, a breathtaking panorama shows the city laid out at the foot of the mountain, sweeping over the narrow streets of Old Montreal to the ocean liners at dock on the magnificent river below.

Quebec Tourist Branch

From Montreal through Quebec City, the majority of Quebec's population resides along the St. Lawrence. The old King's Road on the north shore (now less fancifully called Highway 2) travels the 170 miles between the two cities, passing innumerable little villages on the river banks. Some, like Berthierville and Portneuf draw their living from the tourist trade. These are ancient villages, the first the site of the first Protestant church in Canada and the second a Huron village visited by Cartier. Others, like Ste-Anne-de-la-Pérade, live by fishing. Here a mid-winter festival heralds the river's ice fishing for cod. Midway between Montreal and Quebec City, Trois-Rivières, begun by Champlain in 1615 as a fur trading post, now claims the title of the world's greatest producer of newsprint. It is on the south shore of the St. Maurice River where it empties into the St. Lawrence through three separate channels; hence, the city's name.

Lush spring greenery encircles Port-au-Persil,
a tiny French-Canadian village on the north shore of the St.
Lawrence, in the heart of the Laurentian foothills.

Bonaventure Island, off the Gaspé Peninsula in the Gulf of St. Lawrence, is a windy, rockbound home for thousands of gannets. The parent birds both incubate the single egg and abandon the chick as soon as it develops flight feathers.

All these towns, fronting on their gleaming river, are backed by the foothills of a stunning mountain range. North of the St. Lawrence, the Laurentians stretch from the Ottawa River valley, west of Montreal, to the Saguenay region, east of Quebec City. These mountains are the continent's oldest rocks: monoliths from the Pre-Cambrian past. Glacial ice sheets molded them, curved their peaks, rolled them to smooth mounds, and filled their valleys with unbelievably blue crystalline lakes. Coniferous forests, laced with birch and sugar maple and riddled with trout-choked streams, are the icing for the rounded mountains which become lost in a far distant blue haze. All this is the backyard for the villages of the lower St. Lawrence.

And it is the backyard, too, for Quebec City, undisputedly one of North America's most beautiful and exotic cities. Esconced on the rim of a 350-foot cliff called Cape Diamond, the ancient French city (ninety percent of Quebec's 413,000 people are French-speaking) falls in tiers down the abrupt slope to the wide river below.

Quebec City is called the cradle of Canadian history. Here Cartier spent the winter of 1535; here Champlain founded the settlement in 1608. It is the only walled city on the continent north of Mexico. The thick stone walls were built by the British in the 1820's to protect their huge fortress, the Citadel, atop the cliff. The Citadel is now the summer home of the Governor General of Canada as well as headquarters for the famed French-speaking regiment, 22e Régiment Royal. The Promenade des Gouveneurs descends from the Plains of Abraham, where the French and British fought for possession of Canada in 1759, around the Citadel to Dufferin Terrace, a large park clinging to the cliff side like a sort of balcony for the city. From it, the Lower Town falls away toward the river. Ancient chapels and schools, mansions and convents, little restaurants and pastry shops connected by narrow, crooked streets are products of the seventeenth- and eighteenth-century architecture that gives Quebec City its inimitable charm.

Below the old town, wharves reach into the river to catch ocean ships. Beyond them, on the opposite shore, massive Cape Tourmente tumbles straight into the river. Where the waves gently lap the foot of the mighty ridge, thousands of snow geese, migrating south from Greenland, stop to rest and feed. The rare old homes of the town of Levis cling to the steep cliff and stare back at Quebec City; from here, in 1759, the British bombarded the city. To the rear of Quebec, away from the river, the Laurentians loom northward.

North of Quebec City, the river banks climb even higher as the St. Lawrence cuts through the Laurentian foothills. Sugar maple, hemlock and birch grasp the cliffs, interspersed with poplar, fir and elm. Jack-in-the-pulpit and trilliums shyly peek from beneath the trees and sway in a gentle breeze that hints a salty tang of the ocean. The twenty-mile-long Île d'Orléans in the middle of the river has the quaint charm of the French countryside.

The river broadens in anticipation of its end until, at Baie-St-Paul, fifty miles north of Quebec City, the river is twenty miles across. Cuddled in the hills, Baie-St-Paul watches the hazy south shore, overlooking Île aux Coudres just offshore, where Cartier attended the first Mass ever said in inland Canada.

From Quebec City to the sea, the south shore also wanders through landscapes of incredible grandeur. At St-Jean-Port-Joli, on the southern bank, less than ten miles upriver from Baie-St-Paul on the north, the fresh waters of the Great Lakes give way to the salt of the Atlantic. The river now belongs more to the ocean than to the inland seas. Here the south shore begins a long, gentle curve that forms the northern border of the Gaspé Peninsula.

The villages of the south bank, as with the north, lie cradled in towering cliffs. At Matane, 250 miles north of Quebec and well up the back of the Gaspé, the massive Chic-Choc Mountains, which traverse the peninsula, reach the brink of the mighty river. Chic-Choc is derived from a Micmac word meaning high, sharp points; the massive limestone shards, tinted purple and red, are craggier and taller than the Laurentians. In a thin land bridge, they curve up from Vermont, an extension of the Appalachians.

Tumbling down the sheer sides of the Chic-Chocs, a patchwork of forests and tiny farms tackle the tough earth for meager sustenance. Winding past their feet, through little bays and curving shores, the St. Lawrence River at last releases its waters to the ocean. The great Atlantic tides daily greet the river water, then carry it far to sea; at St-Maurice-de-l'Echourie, near the tip of the Gaspé, low tides can leave fishing boats stranded on their sides.

Inlaid like jewels in the hills on both river banks are the profuse villages of the lower St. Lawrence. This is French country, in language, appearance and traditions, and each tiny village conveys nostalgic qualities from a bygone era.

The typical French-Canadian village has a church at the center, in its very heart, where the steeple can dominate the lesser town buildings. Often these Catholic churches are imitation Gothic; always they reflect the ever-present religion, so deeply embedded in the life of the St. Lawrence. In addition to its church, the typical village proudly protects at least one historic structure whose origins are tied to the town's. The Parish Hall at Cap-St-Ignace, forty miles north of Quebec City, dates back to 1746, and Tadoussac, on the north side of the Saguenay River where it greets the St. Lawrence, has a reconstruction of the Pierre Chauvin house, built in 1599 to become the first French home in Canada.

The houses of the village are built of red brick and wood, close together near the sidewalk. Flanking them, an array of garments on sagging clotheslines flap in the salty breeze. In their backyards, stacks of firewood await the winter that grips French Canada for nine long months.

A few of these towns, like pretty bayside St-Fabien, seventy-five miles south of Matane, are agricultural centers in the midst of hilly farmland. Others, like Baie-Comeau, far up the north shore near the ocean, work in the lumber trade. But most are fishing towns that send fleets deep into the river and onto the ocean as they have done for centuries.

When the catch is in, the fisherman cleans the cod on the village beach while, above him, the gulls wheel and cry, pleading for bits of offal. Rising tall behind the fisherman, should he care to look, are the mountains whose forests reflect green in his village's bay and whose daisies and devil's paintbrush decorate his doorstep. And before him is the river, the mighty partner that gives him his work.

From its birth in the Great Lakes to its death in the Atlantic, the St. Lawrence River links interior North America to the sea. As it is the source of life for the villages of French Canada, it improves the quality of life in far distant ports like Cleveland and Duluth. Through it, they reach the world and the world can answer.

Ports of the Inland Sea

The Great Lakes link together the largest freshwater highway in the world. And, with the opening of the St. Lawrence Seaway, they became an inland extension of the Atlantic Ocean. Many lake cities are seaports, open to nations around the world. Lake country products of iron, timber and grain are directly shipped to Europe, South Africa and China.

Many smaller lake cities do not take part in the seaway trade. They are content with their own products in their smaller harbors. Or they reign as resort meccas for tourists and vacationers from Canada and the United States.

Every city has a personality. Their reasons for living are all their own. Just a few are profiled here.

THUNDER BAY, ONTARIO

The wild country stretches five hundred miles south from Hudson Bay. Pre-Cambrian slabs of the Canadian Shield dam in the violent waters of Lake Superior. Where lake and land meet, geologically ancient cliffs rim the shore. Here, between the wilds of the forest and the lake, is a small oasis of civilization. Here is Thunder Bay.

In 1970, the old communities of Port Arthur and Fort William joined under one new name. Thunder Bay is Ontario's western terminus of the St. Lawrence Seaway and Canada's third largest port. Five miles of breakwaters protect the harbor of Thunder Bay, one of the world's largest grain depots. Nearly 110 million bushels from Canada's Western plains await shipment to the world in the harbor's twenty-four grain elevators. Five million tons of iron ore and over 200,000 tons of newsprint pass through the port each year.

As with most lake cities, fur was the first industry of the Fort William sector of Thunder Bay. In 1679, a post was established here at the mouth of the Kaministiquia River by Daniel Greysolon, sieur Dulhut — a man with a knack for founding Great Lakes ports. Later, Fort William was built (under another name originally) as a major stop on the North West Company route. The Port Arthur sector of Thunder Bay began as an outgrowth of the silver mining once done in the area.

Thunder Bay's attractions go beyond its port. It is the home of Lakehead University, the first in northwest Ontario. In Centennial Park is a 1910-era lumber camp complete with bunkhouse, blacksmith shop and stables. You can even eat a lumberjack's meal — without the sawdust — at the old cookhouse. Sleeping Giant — a magnificent seven-mile-long, thousand-foot-high rock formation jutting into the bay entrance — can be seen from most any point in Thunder Bay. The city is the heart of a fine skiing and hunting area. Trout, muskellunge, sturgeon, kokanee and ouananiche lie in the reedy creeks and cool lake water.

DULUTH, MINNESOTA and SUPERIOR, WISCONSIN

A few traders passed by this way before 1679 when Sieur Dulhut tried to effect a peace with the area's Indians. His name stuck around but he did not. The first permanent settler finally arrived in 1853 and right along with him came the iron-ore rush. Duluth and Superior were iron boom towns from the very beginning, and they still are to a degree. The economy of both cities has risen, fallen and risen again as the iron industry has fluctuated. Their harbor tonnage is surpassed only by New York — and that is only because their lake is closed one-third of the year by ice.

Duluth and Superior are the very westernmost cities on the lakes; they are the seaports farthest inland in the world. The 134,000 residents of the two cities share their twenty-four-mile harbor. A long, narrow breakwater of land crosses the port, creating a near perfect, calm natural harbor.

Begun in the 1600's as a Seneca village, Toronto, Ontario, has become a near-perfect synthesis of Old World and contemporary charms. Its ultra-modern Civic Square is dominated by the arc-shaped City Hall, opened in 1965.

Thomas Erickson

Charles Sheridan

At rest in the icy harbor at Superior, Wisconsin, lake freighters await the spring to resume their duties in the iron trade. Superior shares its harbor with Duluth, Minnesota, and boasts the world's largest ore docks.

Rising 120 feet above the harbor is the Duluth-Superior High Bridge, opened in 1961. The one-and-a-half-mile span joins the two cities and affords a spectacular view of the ocean-going ships passing beneath.

While Duluth is by far the larger of the two cities, Superior has a few "largests" of its own. It boasts the largest ore docks and grain elevators in the world plus the Great Lakes' largest dry docks.

The two cities offer vacationers one to two hundred inches of snow for fine skiing and snowmobiling. At least seventeen shipwrecks lurk in the cold Lake Superior waters awaiting hardy skindivers. City parks on the land breakwater offer miles of sunny beach and sand dunes. Superb fishing and hunting await the sportsman within an hour's drive.

But the greatest pleasure is the look of the land just north of the cities. Volcanic cliffs rise in craggy grandeur six to eight hundred feet over Lake Superior. These giant promontories yield some of the most spectacular scenery anywhere in the lake country. Or anywhere in the world.

SAULT STE. MARIE, MICHIGAN and SAULT STE. MARIE, ONTARIO

Where Lake Superior funnels to its eastern end, a great gurgling river rushes to the lower lakes. The St. Mary's River drops the northern waters twenty-one feet to Lake Huron. Here Canada and the U.S. meet in the two communities of Sault Ste. Marie. Here, too, was a major problem for the upper lake's industries. The iron and copper could not be shipped over the river's rapids. Many days were lost as ships were towed through the streets on rollers or cargo was carried from a ship in Lake Superior to another waiting below the rapids.

Now the "Soo" locks have eradicated the problem. Five ship canals bypass the rapids, carrying more tonnage than any other locks on earth.

In 1671 Father Jacques Marquette established a mission at St. Ignace, Michigan. A simple marker indicates the grave of the great missionary.

Herman Ellis

Sault Ste. Marie, Michigan, on the south side of the locks was the first permanent settlement in Michigan. Father Marquette established a Jesuit mission here in 1670. Today, the city's Tower of History is a monument to the early missionaries who delivered Christianity three hundred years ago. The 210-foot structure yields a commanding view of the twin cities and twenty miles of surrounding northland.

Nearby the locks is an old, many-gabled house, built in 1827, that served as the home and office for Henry Rowe Schoolcraft, famous Indian agent, author and explorer. Schoolcraft's books on Indian lore and legend inspired Henry Wadsworth Longfellow to write his *Song Of Hiawatha*.

The little city is primarily a tourist town. Observation platforms border the locks for a bird's-eye view of their operations. The 550-foot lake freighter *Valley Camp* is docked nearby. Visitors can tour the vessel's engine room, bridge and living spaces. Michigan's Soo is host to the International 500 — one of the biggest events in snowmobiling.

Sault Ste. Marie, Ontario, is two minutes away via the International Bridge, opened in 1962, and engineered by the same man who built the Mackinac Bridge. It spans the locks for another fine view

of lake and ocean freighters lifting and lowering as tons of water rush in and out of the locks. The Ontario city is the larger of the two and the more industrial. It has Canada's second largest steel mill as well as ship-building yards and paper mills.

Both cities offer a natural treasure trove to vacationers, such as the St. Mary's River, which is rife with walleye and Northern pike.

ST. IGNACE and MACKINAW CITY, MICHIGAN

St. Ignace is quiet now, its few thousand residents content in their delightful wilderness surroundings. But in the early days of French civilization, St. Ignace was big business. Two Indian villages (Huron and Ottawa), the mission established by Father Marquette in 1671, palisaded Fort De Baude and a fur trader's colony made the cosmopolitan community the leading settlement in Michigan. Set on the Straits of Mackinac, St. Ignace was a port of call for the fur trade as well as French, British and American armies. Across the straits, the little community at Mackinaw City gathered its own rich share of the fur trade.

After a community was established at Fort Pontchartrain in Detroit, the focus turned away from St. Ignace. When Fort Michilimackinac was erected at Mackinaw City around 1750, this village further diminished St. Ignace's importance. The British ruled the fort after the French, suffering an Indian massacre of the garrison in 1763. The reconstructed Fort Michilimackinac stands today as Mackinaw City's foremost site.

Mackinaw City is a busy little resort town with fewer than one thousand year-round residents. Rows of restaurants, fudge shops and souvenir stores dominate its two main streets. The opening of the Mackinac Bridge in 1959 has somewhat revitalized St. Ignace, and the sleepy fishing village now supports an active tourist trade. Visitors enjoy its little museum of local history, ancient Indian cemetery and monument to Father Marquette.

Both St. Ignace and Mackinaw City offer ferries to Mackinac Island, so thousands of sightseers pass through their streets. The annual Labor Day Bridge Walk attracts thousands more; two lanes of "Mighty Mac" are closed to motor traffic while hikers hoof the five-mile span. The breathtaking view of both Michigan peninsulas, lakes Huron and Michigan, the straits' islands and lake freighters make the bridge walk a favorite of camera and scenery buffs.

Both towns are steeped in history; they keep their pasts alive in annual festivities. St. Ignace uses the few days preceding the bridge walk for its Black Gown Tree pageant. ("Black gown tree" was

Herman Ellis

*Once an important fur post, Mackinaw City has
traded in its pelts for gift shops and restaurants.
The little resort annually reenacts the 1763 massacre at Fort
Michilimackinac. In the background is the Mackinac Bridge
which connects Michigan's Upper and Lower peninsulas.*

an Indian term for the Cross — the missionary, in
his black robes, made his Cross of a tree limb tied
horizontally to a cut off tree trunk.) The pageant
reenacts Father Marquette's life and founding of
St. Ignace, the second oldest community in Michigan. Mackinaw City has an annual pageant of its
own, as villagers, in eighteenth-century costume,
reenact the 1763 massacre at Fort Michilimackinac.

St. Ignace and Mackinaw City both offer their
lush pine and hardwood backdrops as a superior
vacationland. The color tours in the fall north
woods are unequalled anywhere on earth.

GREEN BAY, WISCONSIN

Duluth means iron. Gary, steel. When you talk
Mackinaw City, you talk tourists. And Green Bay
is the Packers.

The little city (population: about 88,000) lives
its football team; it is a city-owned, city-loved
business. The team's name honors one of Green

Bay's other big money makers, the meat-packing
plants. From the earliest practice in July to the last
game in December (or in Green Bay's case, often
the championships in January), the city is alive
with a spirit that tops the big football towns.

Green Bay can claim another honor, too; it is a
center of Midwest history. Jean Nicolet came
across the area on his way to China back in 1634
(not many years after the Pilgrims moved in on
Plymouth Rock). Missionaries and fur traders were
here by the early 1700's. The initial permanent
settler arrived in 1745 to plant the first farm west
of Detroit. Green Bay is the oldest settlement in
Wisconsin, and for years it was a busy branch of
the North West Company.

The community has preserved its history well.
Seven old homes (one the oldest in Wisconsin) are
now museums, furnished with the possessions of
their original owners and pieces of the same period.

Milwaukee Journal

*Thick chunks of ice, broken
and fitted together like pieces of a
giant jigsaw puzzle, line the Lake
Michigan shore at Milwaukee.*

The Beer City's neighborhoods are rife with old world culture. It brews more beer than any other city, but its biggest industry is machinery manufacturing. The craftsmen are among the world's finest. Their trade was brought to America three and four generations ago by northern Europeans and has been passed along to each new crop of Milwaukeeans.

Defeated revolutionists from Germany arrived in the mid-nineteenth century to form an intellectual and cultural center. The Socialist Party grew and took office by 1910. Milwaukee today has a reputation for the cleanest big city government and lowest crime rate.

Over 700,000 residents in America's twelfth largest city can enjoy one of the finest museums of natural history in the entire lake country. Milwaukee's Performing Arts Center, home of the city's symphony orchestra and theater groups, is a handsome new complex, completed in 1969. The three glass domes of Mitchell Park Conservatory house vegetation of the earth's three climates — arid, tropical and temperate. Along with Chicago, it has one of the finest zoos in the world.

Milwaukee's harbor handles six million tons of cargo every year. The city leads the world in the production of electrical apparatus and gasoline and Diesel engines.

The city's many fine restaurants and annual Summerfest and Old Milwaukee Days celebrations are responsible for Milwaukee's good natured, genial, kindly atmosphere. *Gemuetlichkeit.*

All seven houses plus one old Moravian church are included in the National Register of Historic Places. The city also offers the National Railroad Museum — one of the best known in the country for railroading memorabilia. Green Bay is definitely a delight for antique lovers.

However, the city has not let its story end with a novel history. It is one of the fastest growing cities in the state. Shipyards, limestone quarries and paper manufacturing keep the inland seaport bustling. Surrounded by dairy lands, it leads the nation in the processing of cheese.

History and cheese, paper and railroads. But when you think of Green Bay, think of the Packers, because that is where the city's spirit lies.

MILWAUKEE, WISCONSIN

Gemuetlichkeit. That's German for geniality, kindliness, good nature. And that's English for Milwaukee.

CHICAGO, ILLINOIS

Chicago — enthusiastic and powerful, ambitious and strong. But it wasn't always so. The city was in no hurry to grow up. A small mission was built in 1674 but little progress was made until Fort Dearborn appeared in 1803. In the intermittent 129 years, a few explorers and fur traders journeyed through but the first permanent settler did not arrive until 1770. A black Haitian businessman, Jean Pointe De Sable, built his home and trading post on the north shore of the Chicago River.

When the city finally began to grow, it boomed. The population quadrupled in the decade between 1837 and 1847. Its rapid construction was of wood; the drought of 1871 helped Mrs. O'Leary's cow ignite the tinderbox town. The blaze razed seventeen thousand buildings; three hundred residents perished. Today, the famous old water tower stands downtown as a remnant of the great Chicago fire.

*At night the lights of Lake Shore Drive (above)
outline Chicago's waterfront; beside the drive, lovely
Lincoln Park decorates the north shore. An ocean freighter
(right), having navigated the St. Lawrence Seaway and four
of the Great Lakes, steams into Chicago's harbor.*

The city rebuilt above its ashes fast and strong. The country's first skyscraper soared a magnificent ten stories tall in 1885. The country's tallest has just appeared — the Sears Tower's 110 stories rising 1,450 feet to crown the city. John Hancock Center and the Standard Oil Building stand just below it.

From the emporiums of Old Town through the exclusive shops of North Michigan Avenue to the giant department stores of the Loop, Chicago is a shopper's paradise. Music lovers flock to the world famous Chicago Symphony. And museum fans can have a field day. The Chicago Art Institute holds more French Impressionist paintings than the Louvre and the Field Museum of Natural History is among the country's finest. The Museum of Science and Industry displays a real submarine and a working coal mine. The Shedd Aquarium is the world's largest; Lincoln Park's Oriental gardens rival Japan's.

The Chicago port is one of the lake's busiest. The gigantic Navy Pier alone can handle six ships at a time. This, and the Illinois Waterway to the Mississippi, combine to make Illinois the largest exporting state in the nation. Outside the port area, the Chicago lakefront is a recreational haven for the city's 3.3 million dwellers. For many miles, parks, beaches, yacht basins and public buildings line the shore. Chicago has its homely neighborhoods, but its shoreline is the prettiest city scenery on the lakes.

GARY, INDIANA

Gary is the city steel built. Its population today is 175,000; in 1905, its population was 0.

The Jesuits paddled back and forth in the area but built no missions and saved no souls. A solitary fur trader built his home (it still stands a few miles east of Gary) but no one joined him. Potawatomi Indians ruled the area until they left their villages for Western reservations.

Then, in 1905, along came Judge Elbert H. Gary, chairman of U.S. Steel. He had a dream of a

170

steel plant, the world's largest. He wanted it on the lake, midway between the iron fields to the north and the coal fields to the south. Residents of the posh Waukegan, Illinois, lakefront will be horrified to know Judge Gary seriously considered their pastoral village for his steel mill. However, the twelve thousand unoccupied, cheap acres at Lake Michigan's southern shore finally won his attention. So there Judge Gary built a city — the largest in the U.S. with totally twentieth-century origins.

The lake's sandy shore was moved out; topsoil was railroaded in. In three and a half years the mill was built and steel began to pour. In a very few months, a city of tar paper shacks was built to house thousands of steel workers and their families. Facilities improved as Polish, Czech and Ukrainian immigrants continued to pour into the mill. The World War II labor shortage brought blacks from the south, Appalachian hill people and Mexican laborers.

Other industries grew to support and serve the queen bee, steel. Gary is now in the heart of one of the largest industrial areas on earth. Five more steel companies on the Indiana shore ring Gary's U.S. Steel operations.

DETROIT, MICHIGAN and WINDSOR, ONTARIO

What most people know about Detroit is that it is big, it is the Motor City, it is industrial and there is no reason to go there.

It is big — 1.5 million residents make it America's fifth largest city — and it is indeed the Motor City. The auto industry grew up right along with Detroiters like Henry Ford, Walter Chrysler, Ransom E. Olds and the Fisher brothers. It is also true that Detroit is industrial; even excluding the auto industry, Detroit plants hire more workers than all the manufacturers in Boston, Cleveland or Baltimore.

But the city is much more than this.

The seventy-five-acre Detroit Civic Center is now the hub of the city. Bordering the riverfront, its plaza offers a park where picnickers can watch the overseas traffic of the world's busiest river.

James Marchael — Van Cleve Photography

With exhibits like a captured German submarine, a working coal mine and a walk-in construct of a human heart, Chicago's Museum of Science and Industry on the lakefront has become one of America's most heavily visited museums.

Cobo Hall/Cobo Arena stretches over seventeen riverfront acres of the Civic Center. The exhibit areas alone in this modern convention center are so huge that eight football games could be played at the same time. A riverfront walkway with a view of the marina skirts the hall and arena. The Veterans Memorial Building, built where Antoine de la Mothe Cadillac first landed in 1701, the City-County Building, and the Henry and Edsel Ford Auditorium, home of the Detroit Symphony Orchestra, also grace the Civic Center grounds.

A short walk away, a new $500 million riverfront complex of office and apartment buildings is being developed. A main objective of this development is to further beautify the shoreline.

Detroit offers the unique as well as the new. A money museum features twelve thousand coins and primitive money forms — furs to beetle shells. The *J. W. Wescott II* is a mailboat with its own zipcode; it delivers mail to the vessels passing through the twenty-nine-mile Detroit River. Belle Isle, in the Detroit River, is a lovely park. Acres of virgin forest harbor a fallow deer herd and inland lakes and ponds dot the island.

Not far from Detroit is Greenfield Village and Henry Ford Museum. The village contains nearly one hundred homes, workshops (including Thomas Edison's) and public buildings moved from all over the nation and rearranged in a picturesque early American town. The museum contains acres of Americana — furniture to aircraft to two hundred antique cars.

Just across the river from Detroit is Windsor, Canada's southernmost metropolis. This is the only place in Canada where you have to look north to see the United States. Windsor lies on an arm of land that curls beneath Michigan.

Once upon a time pioneer French farmers settled Windsor. The rich soil and temperate climate of the area still enable Windsor to claim the title of Ontario's market garden. In an earlier day, the city did a magnificent "rum-running" business; fine distillery and brewery goods remain a major contribution of the city to the world. But Windsor is best known as Canada's automotive manufacturing center.

The Francois Baby home, the oldest standing brick dwelling on the Detroit River, is a national historic site; it is now a museum of pioneer and Indian life. The Art Gallery of Windsor is renowned for its extensive collection of Eskimo sculpture, Canada's native art.

Two tunnels and a suspension bridge link Windsor to Detroit. Windsor is the main port of entry into Canada for U.S. citizens. More than 17 million travelers cross the boundary between these international twin cities each year.

TOLEDO, OHIO

Toledo is a glass city. The discovery of natural gas and oil south of the city led to the beginnings of an enormous glass industry in the 1880's. Today four major glass-product companies headquartered here turn out everything from tableware to windshields. The Toledo Museum of Art features an extensive glass collection dating from when man first started making it, 4,500 years ago.

The city's second major breadwinner is refining. Pipelines deliver crude oil from as far as Texas and Wyoming to three giant refineries. These process more than eight million barrels a month.

Toledo lives on the Maumee, the largest river flowing into the Great Lakes. Its harbor stretches from the coal and iron-ore facilities at the mouth of the Maumee to a point seven miles upriver. Giant grain elevators and overseas cargo terminals line the river banks. Raw rubber comes in from Singapore; Toledo-made jeeps go out for South Africa. The foreign trade zone is the Great Lakes' only operating free port. Here, import goods can be stored technically outside U.S. boundaries on a duty deferred basis.

Toledo is a gateway to the Lake Erie islands' vacation havens. A nationally respected zoo (begun

Working hard to upgrade its image, Detroit is piercing its skyline with many new riverfront buildings. The city began in 1701 as the site of a fort built on a strategic détroit, or strait.

City of Detroit

173

City of Detroit

in 1899 with the donation of a woodchuck), a hundred city parks, golf courses and yacht clubs service the community.

But Toledo's Great Lake is dying; some say it may already be dead. Like all Lake Erie cities, Toledo must now take extra care. Or the source of its life, the transporter of its goods, will be nothing but an open sewer.

CLEVELAND, OHIO

Moses Cleaveland dropped by long enough to plat a city in 1796, but Lorenzo Carter settled it. From then until recently, very little could be said about Cleveland.

But now the city is undergoing a cultural renaissance. Its downtown University Circle is a five-hundred-acre expanse of parks and gardens.

Within this pastoral setting are a first-rate university, law school, hospital and the renowned Cleveland Institute of Art. Severance Hall, one of the world's most acoustically perfect buildings, houses the famous Cleveland Orchestra. Many critics believe this orchestra to be the finest in the country.

Cleveland is a center of human progress in more than its cultural life. It is noted for prominent medical research; open-heart surgery techniques were pioneered here. Here, too, is the NASA Lewis Research Center.

The city is also a leading steel producer. Its port delivers iron to its mills and transports coal to the upper lakes. Paint and apparel, paper and leather goods are all products of the nation's tenth largest city. Thirteen thousand acres of parks ring the city's industrial core.

174

*The Spirit of Detroit (opposite) rises before the City-
County Building; Detroiters have nicknamed this sculpture the Green
Giant. The Maumee River (above), the largest river flowing into
the Great Lakes, courses through the heart of Toledo, Ohio.*

ERIE, PENNSYLVANIA

Pennsylvania's only Great Lakes port is one of the best. The Presque Isle peninsula juts out from the mainland, hooks around and forms a calm, landlocked harbor. Over two thousand vessels enter it each year, delivering iron from Minnesota and pulp wood from Canada, and hauling coal to the upper lakes.

The city began in 1753 with a French fort on Presque Isle. The British then occupied the fort until the Senecas burned it a decade after its construction. During the Civil War, Erie was a major station on the Underground Railroad.

The city grew up as a shipbuilding center. Its industrious little yard sent the bulk of Commodore Oliver Hazard Perry's fleet into the Battle of Lake Erie in the War of 1812. The *Wolverine*, the world's first all-iron battleship, steamed out of Erie's harbor in 1843.

Today Erie, stretching out on a plain a hundred feet above the Lake Erie level, is yet another Great Lakes' industrial center. The laborers among its 129,000 residents manufacture boilers, stoves, plastics and engines. The city's chief commerce is in iron ore, lumber, coal, petroleum and grain.

Perry's flagship, the reconstructed *Niagara*, can be seen on the city's lakefront, and the home that Perry lived in while his fleet was built is also open to the public. The Presque Isle peninsula is now a state park so the city is rimmed with a pretty recreation area. Erie residents find it a welcome relief from their city's industrial environs.

Ninety-acre Ontario Place, built on man-made islands in Lake Ontario, houses exhibits on the province's history and is one of the many attractions in Toronto.

BUFFALO, NEW YORK

Where the waters of eastern Lake Erie rumble off to Lake Ontario via the Niagara River, La Salle launched his tiny ship *Griffin* in 1679. So Buffalo's first business was shipbuilding. But after La Salle sailed away, nobody wanted Buffalo until almost a century later. Then the French settled down, but the British pushed them out again a year later. The settlement made a third try at existence but the British burned it down in the War of 1812; its five hundred disgruntled settlers took to the woods.

Maybe settlers would have just given up on the bad luck location had it not been chosen as the western end of "Clinton's Big Ditch," the Erie Canal. The canal's completion in 1825 ushered in an era of uninhibited growth; the eventual advent of cheap power from Niagara Falls touched off an industrial rampage.

Today Buffalo's 460,000 people reside in one of the country's most diversified industrial complexes. Meat is packed, flour milled. Publishers and printers supply each other; steel is poured while planes and furniture are built.

Buffalo is a seedbed of Presidential trivia. Theodore Roosevelt took oath here after McKinley was shot at the city's Pan-American Exposition. Millard Fillmore died here, ending an undistinguished political career. And Grover Cleveland was once the Buffalo mayor.

TORONTO, ONTARIO

You can tour Europe in Toronto. Dozens of nationalities create a mosaic of ethnic neighborhoods. Folk festivals are an active part of Toronto life. Thirty percent of all Ontario residents live in their capital city; that's ten percent of all Canadians. It is about the fastest growing of all the Great Lakes' cities.

Toronto history has meshed with its modern; its pollution controls took an early hand in managing its industrial growth. And an active waterfront plan is constantly beautifying the shore. Toronto is the hub of Ontario industry, but you will probably remember the city best by its parks.

A necklace of islands, the Toronto Islands, ring the city's Lake Ontario bay. Ferries interweave with the islands, dropping sightseers for sunny days at the island beaches and shores.

From mid-August to Labor Day, Toronto hosts the Canadian National Exhibition — the world's largest and oldest continuing fair. The midway, fireworks, bandshell and grandstand entertain three million visitors.

Just offshore from Exhibition Park is a fabulous new ninety-acre complex on man-made islands. Ontario Place houses exhibits on Ontario history and features a film festival, marina, amphitheater and picnic grounds. Another new symbol of Toronto growth is the City Hall, a stunning sample of modern architecture.

What is old is as vital as what is new in Toronto. The city's oldest habitation, the Scadding Cabin, stands in Exhibition Park. Built in 1794, the little home is decorated with period furnishings. Also open to the public is the William Lyon Mackenzie House, home of the "little Rebel," Toronto's first mayor. And Casa Loma, the only castle of its kind anywhere in North America, graces the city with Old World opulence.

With ninety-five thousand square miles of sparkling blue water in the inland seas, a captain can sail on forever. All the Great Lakes' cities are ports for little boats as well as the mighty ships. Here, sailboats leisurely cruise on Lake Ontario near Rochester, New York.

ROCHESTER, NEW YORK

What cherry blossoms are to Washington, lilacs are to Rochester. Each spring, fifty thousand tourists visit the city's parks and gardens during its week long Lilac Festival. The original lilacs were brought to New England by the earliest colonists. They were a symbol of good luck and a reminder of home. Rochester now harbors hundreds of varieties and has the world's largest display. Hence, its nickname, the Flower City.

In addition to lilacs, Rochester (population close to 300,000) is a photography town. Eastman Kodak Company is headquartered here, manufacturing a wide range of photographic equipment. Eastman's name, a legend in the Flower City, is also connected with the famous Eastman School of Music, Eastman Theater, and the internationally known Eastman House of Photography.

Rochester was well settled by the early 1800's. Later Susan B. Anthony lived here, and the former home of this early women's-rights defender is now open to the public. Here, too, the great black leader, Frederick Douglass, carried on his anti-slavery work. The city offers a fabulous new computerized planetarium and a unique downtown shopping center that is all under one roof.

Rochester is an old city, so if you come to Rochester, see it at lilac time. Then the colorful parks help hide an old city's wrinkles.

The Fate
of the Lakes

All lakes die. It is a perfectly natural process called eutrophication. Inflowing waters deposit sediments on lake bottoms, making the lakes shallower. As they get shallower, they get warmer; coldwater fish desert them. Waters also carry in nutrients so algae thrive. As they die, they fill the lakes with decomposed organic matter so the lakes become shallower still. Sunlight is then able to penetrate down to the bottoms and plants take root. Eventually, the lakes become swamps and the swamps become dry land.

This is normal. Nature has killed millions of lakes this way; others, it has destroyed by glaciers. But this process should require hundreds and hundreds of years.

Man is successfully accomplishing the same thing in very few decades. And that is not natural at all.

The problem is simply that there are too many people for the Great Lakes to handle. Pollution is the natural consequence. It is aging the lakes at least ten times faster than normal; we are polluting our waters to an early death. Lakes Erie and Ontario plus the southern end of Lake Michigan are the most noticeably affected. Geologically they are all very young lakes, but because of man, they are now middle-aged to old.

Carp are replacing the whitefish in Lake Michigan; many state parks along Lake Erie have closed their beaches. If you wish to swim in Lake Ontario, you often must walk through a slimy green scum simply to reach the water. Lake Huron, still rather clean, is being badgered by industrial air pollution. Lake Superior has such an infertile rocky basin, it is difficult for growth to begin. But it, too, is threatened by the wastes of one enormous mining concern.

Fortunately, Lake Superior is still nearly pure. Its waters are fed into all the other lakes, and there would be no hope of purging them should Superior become foul. In addition, the upper lake is so huge (and it has only one major drainage area) that it takes anywhere from two to five centuries to change its waters completely. And just one flushing would not totally remove all pollutants. So if we dirty it, hundreds of years would be required to make it pure again.

The problems for Lake Michigan are similar but more immediate. It has only two major drainage

(continued on page 181)

Someone had a good time on this Lake Superior beach; due to the beer bottles and cans they left, no one else will. Many Lake Erie beaches must be cleared of this kind of refuse every day.

Joe Kirkish

areas so it requires well over a century to flush. Like Superior, its waters drain through the lower lakes. Not too slowly and very surely, the polluted waters of Lake Michigan's southern end can spread to the north, through the Straits of Mackinac and into Lake Huron. Huron's waters recycle in twenty years, Ontario's in eight and Erie's in less than three. So dirty Lake Erie would be flushed clean in relatively short time if all polluting influences could be halted. Until they are curtailed, however, Lake Ontario will never be clean, for eighty-five percent of its water comes from Lake Erie.

To put it simply, four kinds of pollution are threatening the Great Lakes — population, agricultural, industrial and air.

People pollution began with the first lakefront settlers. Sewage was channeled directly into the lakes. However, the lakes could cope with that because there were so few people. Microorganisms in the water broke the sewage down into inorganic chemicals; these fertilized aquatic vegetation. The plants then produced oxygen and became fish food. A limited amount of human excrement can be assimilated into the natural life cycle of the Great Lakes.

But millions of people now live around the Great Lakes and thousands of tons of sewage solids are flushed into the waters each day. In the more advanced of communities today, sewage treatment removes most solids and converts the organic matters to inorganic chemicals. Unfortunately, these chemicals are good fertilizers, as good as the original raw sewage. The consequence is that algae is taking over the lakes. It reproduces at incredible rates; at times, four million algae have been found in every quart of Lake Erie water. The decomposition of these plants takes the oxygen from the water, killing fish and other aquatic life. It is the slimy remains of algae that coats many beaches, smelling almost as bad as the sewage did.

The effects of people pollution include our product wastes. Beer cans, plastic cartons and discarded tires are almost as common as sand on many Great Lakes beaches. Every year Americans throw away seventy-four billion bottles and cans. To complicate the problem, there is not only more waste but it is more destructive now because many of today's miracle fabrics are not readily biode-

When pollutants and lampreys killed off the larger fish in Lake Michigan in the late 1960's, the smaller food fish, alewives, overpopulated and died, covering beaches with their carrion. Since then coho salmon and trout have been re-introduced and the alewife problem has abated.

gradable. What man has made often cannot be naturally broken back down into the elements normally found in and unharmful to the earth and lakes. So our modern wastes will be with us for centuries.

Even those who enjoy the wilderness often damage it with their vehicles. Almost everyone knows automobiles are an enormous pollution problem; fewer realize that their motorboats leave behind oil wastes in the lakes. Snowmobiles and four-wheel-drive vehicles tear the forest and disrupt wildlife when improperly used. New York has banned their use in sections of many forest preserves. Other all-terrain vehicles, especially dune buggies, are deadly to small trees and low shrubs. They destroy the plant cover on dunes so nothing holds the sands in place. Working at these rips in the dunes, winds dig away "blow-out" areas which keep expanding once they have begun. Consequently, even small tears in the ground cover can eventually destroy the dune.

It is ironic that our attempt to be clean is causing one of the Great Lakes' dirtiest problems. However, huge quantities of detergents are sudsing their way through disposal plants. Their phosphate base makes an excellent fertilizer that further increases the algae count. The chemicals that are being used to replace the phosphates are not yet well tested; no one is sure about how much damage they may do.

Agricultural pollution is also taking its toll on the Great Lakes. Manure from large concentrations of farm animals is flushed into the water network and chemical fertilizers drain into the lakes. The insecticides that wash into the water are extremely stable and do not easily break down. Their longevity makes them highly dangerous. Enough DDT has been found in many Great Lakes fish and the gulls that eat them to render both sterile. Insecticides have afflicted every link of the life chain in the Great Lakes' area. Even the bald eagle, our national bird, has fallen under its ill effects. In fact, the higher on the chain the more harmful, because the chemical's effect multiplies as it passes from animal to animal.

Like sewage, industrial dumping began years ago when few businesses operated near the Great Lakes. Now, such a massive concentration of factories work in this industrial core that the lakes can no longer handle them. They add to the water an amount of substances that have the effect of fertilizers equal to the amount from sewage. These substances intensify the algal growth and depletion

Joe Kirkish

of oxygen for the higher life forms. Since only a tiny fraction of a percent of water is dissolved oxygen, it would not be, unfortunately, too difficult to remove all of it in this way. Then all life in the Great Lakes would cease.

Beyond industrial fertilizers come the poisonous effects of wastes like arsenic, cyanide and lead. Twice the acceptable amount of mercury poison has been found in the lakes' fish and fowl. No one is sure how much damage these poisons will do or when their effects will be dissipated; estimates run over one hundred years. Another unknown factor is how badly the lakes are being damaged by companies that use the water for cooling, then run it back into the lakes at a higher temperature than

surrounding lake water. This is called thermal pollution. What is known is that a temperature rise of even a few degrees can kill several species of Great Lakes' fish as well as promote algal growth.

Oil is the most obvious pollution because it can easily be seen; that does not necessarily make it the worst, but it does attract a lot of attention. Because oil floats on the surface, it disrupts the oxygen-making process, so it destroys beaches and fish. The slick coats waterfowl, penetrating their feathers and causing them to lose their buoyancy. Very soon, they drown. In 1969, the oil slick on Cleveland's Cuyahoga River was so bad, the river actually caught fire. Two bridges were damaged before the flames were doused. Now Cleveland

The open burning that is still allowed in the dumps of Michigan's Keweenaw Peninsula is as bad on the eyes as it is on the air. The time is soon approaching when even the most remote woodland communities must find healthier methods of garbage disposal.

fireboats must patrol it because the waterway is considered a fire hazard.

Industrial air pollution is yet another demon for the Great Lakes. Much of what is carried in the air will eventually end up in the lakes. For instance, metal smelters belch poisonous sulfurs into the air and all the vegetation near the works dies. That includes the valuable aquatic vegetation that sustains millions of fish. The little lakes around Ontario's Georgian Bay are now suffering under this kind of pollution. How much damage is being done is anybody's guess.

What oil is to water pollution, a temperature inversion is to air pollution. It is highly visible and can be deadly.

An extended period of calm sunny weather, the kind we like, brings on the worst of these inversions. Then the human death rate can become a good deal higher than normal. What happens to create an inversion is this:

The sun warms the calm air during the day. At night, the earth loses part of its heat through radiation. This makes the lower layer of air next to the earth cooler than the stagnant warm air above it. Because the lower air is cooler, it will not rise, so the warmer layer acts as a sort of lid. The layer is called a temperature inversion because it is more normal for air temperature to decrease with increasing altitude.

Not only is the colder air held in but so are the smokes, fumes and gases from our industries and automobiles. They continue to build up until they form a visible gray blanket of poisons hugging the earth and dropping into the lakes. They remain until a strong enough wind can break up the inversion situation. Because so many cities now rim the Great Lakes, these temperature inversions are no longer rare.

Perhaps the lake pollution story can most graphically be described through the tale of Lake Erie. This Great Lake is by far the dirtiest; the polluted future of all the rest can be foretold in it, if the situation on the other lakes is not improved. By heeding its warnings, we may avoid the same fate for the others.

Lake Erie is the most polluted for two primary reasons. First, an enormous concentration of population rims its shores; it is the dumping ground for cities like Toledo, Cleveland, Erie, Buffalo and Detroit (just upriver from it). Second, Erie's own geography did not give it much of a chance against man's fuels, smokes and sewage.

The lake is extremely shallow; it averages less than sixty feet. Its basin was dug by glaciers in silty, shifting clay. The lake's surrounding shores were weak and readily collapsed under the easily stirred waves of the shallow lake. These quicksilver shores became a fine, moist marshland, abundant in forage and protection for waterfowl. As described in Chapter 8, a few marshy remnants remain today, but they once ringed the whole lake. Enormous hordes of mayflies blackened the skies as they swarmed into the wild marshes. They were such an endless food supply that Lake Erie built up the greatest concentration of freshwater fish the world has ever known. So great was this abundance of fish that early settlers merely stood near pools on the lakeshore and stabbed them with pitchforks or slashed them with axes. Three-hundred-pound

Pollution from nickel smelting plants (below) is quickly spreading to Lake Huron, killing any vegetation in its path. An unfinished house (opposite) in Bayside, Wisconsin, slips toward Lake Michigan as wind and high water erode away the bluff.

Joe Kirkish

sturgeon became tangled in and destroyed the fish nets so fishermen gathered them, stacked them in piles and burned them on the shores.

Paradoxically, the same marshy shores that provided so much life for Lake Erie and its vicinity eventually helped to destroy it. When the forests were felled, Lake Erie became the center of a great farmland. However, with the demise of a system of tree roots, nothing held the unstable land in place. A flood of silt carried topsoils, sewage and clay into Lake Erie. Every stream mouth was choked; everywhere, the weak shoreline collapsed.

Along the shores, fish began to die out. The silt was coating their spawning reefs, suffocating their eggs. Great swirls of dirt billowing into the lake kept sunlight from penetrating the water. The aquatic plants near the shore that required light could no longer grow, so the food for plant-eating fish was gone. As vegetation died away, so did the insect swarms. And so, too, did insect-eating fish. Fish that preyed on smaller fish could no longer see through the dirt well enough to hunt. The billions of tons of silt that barreled into Lake Erie effectively destroyed every source of fish food. Only deep in the lake, far from the silt storms, could any kind of fish life continue.

All this happened well before 1900. Industrial pollution had not even begun to take its enormous toll, yet life was already deserting Lake Erie.

When agricultural and industrial pollutants did enter the scene, they eliminated the life deep in the lake. The chemicals promoted algae that robbed the lake of oxygen. More valuable aquatic plants were replaced by scum; the remaining mayfly larvae beds suffocated. The few fish that had lived through the silt storms now died or moved on to other more pleasant lakes. As an example, in 1955, more than 19.5 million pounds of blue pike were caught in the lake; since 1960 — only five years later — records show that only one blue pike has been taken from the lake.

The silt had smothered, but dirt could have eventually been dissipated; life could have returned. However, many of the man-made chemicals are actually poisonous. Some say Lake Erie could be cleaned at a cost of billions of dollars; others maintain that the effects of poisons can never be removed. All we know for sure is that Erie's shores are slimy, its beaches are closed, its fish are dead.

Today, there are eighty-nine endangered species of wildlife; the ninetieth is man. To save ourselves, we must save our earth. And men *are* trying. Millions of dollars are being spent by industries to find effective solutions to their dust, fumes and run-offs (only a handful of companies pretend to an inalienable right to dump whatever, wherever they wish). Cities are experimenting with improved methods of sewage disposal. The Canadian and United States governments are united in tightening regulations for the lakes and in finding effective insecticides and fertilizers that do not destroy what they should not destroy. People are more conscious of their own wastes; many are discovering what refuse containers are for.

As we have judged our fathers for the state we are in, so shall our children judge us. Let us not leave them diseased waters and foul air. Instead, let us leave a legacy of Great Lakes cleaner than when we arrived.

An increasing number of old fishing boats are being left to rot on the Great Lakes' shores. Such derelicts are more than eyesores: Although the wood will eventually decay, the bolts, nails and other metal parts will not.

Joe Kirkish

Photo by Linda B. Myers

"Father of Lakes!" Thy waters bend
Beyond the gull's utmost view,
When, throned in heaven, he sees Thee send
Back to the sky its world of blue.

APPENDIX

	Lake Superior	Lake Michigan	Lake Huron	Lake St. Clair	Lake Erie	Lake Ontario
Areas (square miles)						
Water surface, United States	20,600	22,300	9,150	198	4,980	3,560
Water surface, Canada	11,100	—	13,900	292	4,930	3,990
TOTAL	31,700	22,300	23,050	490	9,910	7,550
Maximum Depth (feet)	1,333	923	750	21	210	802
Average Depth (feet)	489	279	195	10	62	283
Volume of Water (cubic miles)	2,935	1,180	849	1	116	393
Length of Coastline (miles) (including islands)	2,980	1,660	3,180	169	856	726
Mean Elevation (feet)	600.4	578.7	578.7	573	570.4	244.8
Average Seasonal Depth Fluctuation (feet)	1.1	1.1	1.1	1.6	1.5	1.8
Mean Outflow (cubic feet/second)	75,000	52,000	187,000	188,000	202,000	239,000

Length of Outflow Rivers (miles)	
St. Mary's	70
St. Clair	27
Detroit	32
Niagara	37
St. Lawrence	502

The relative sizes and depths of the Great Lakes to each other are shown in this diagram. Unlike any of the other lakes, Lake Ontario is very deep in relation to its surface area.

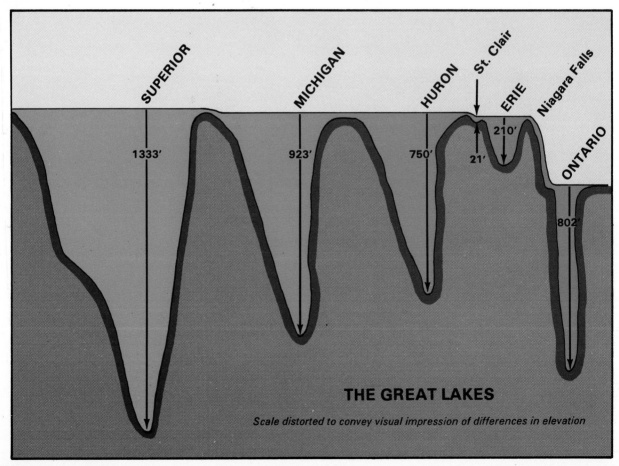

THE GREAT LAKES

Scale distorted to convey visual impression of differences in elevation

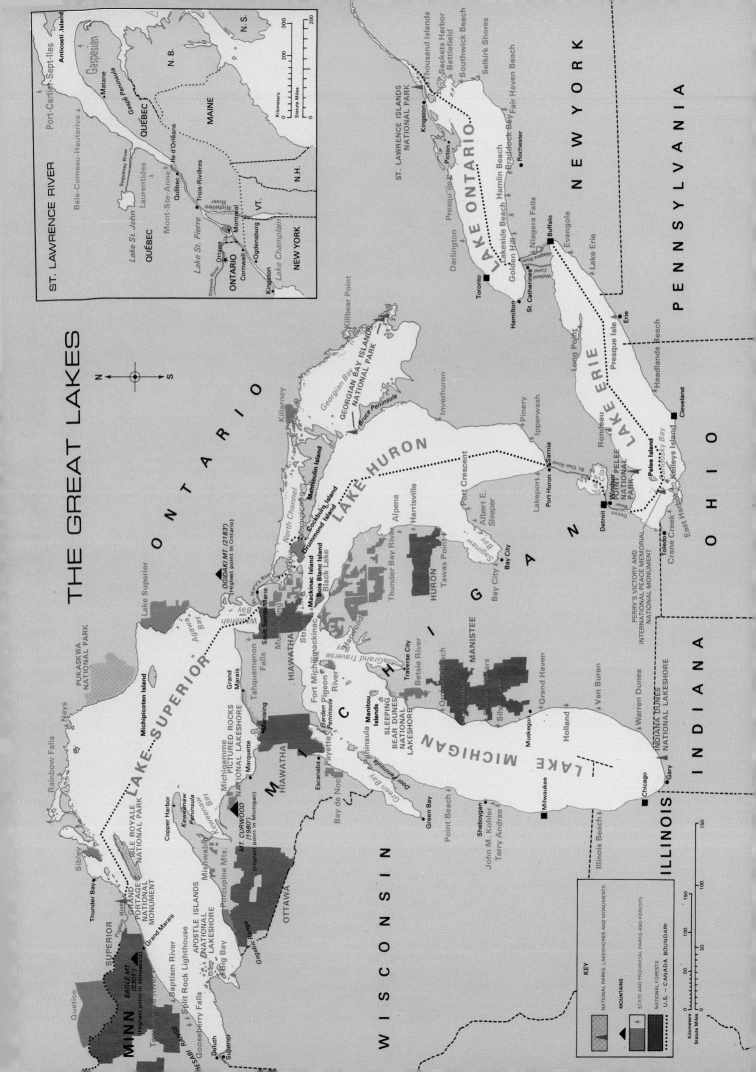

INDEX

Italicized numbers refer to illustrations.

Abbreviations: N.F. – National Forest; N.L. – National Lakeshore; N.P. – National Park;
P.P. – Provincial Park; S.F. – State Forest; S.P. – State Park.